Step
by Step
PHONICS®

Makes Reading and Spelling Easy
A Comprehensive Literacy Program for All Beginning Readers

Laurie Lee Bell
Moorhead State University, Minnesota

Back to the Basics Publishing
Rancho Cucamonga, California

Step by Step Phonics® Makes Reading and Spelling Easy

Copyright © 1994, 1998 by Laurie Lee Bell
Completely Revised Edition

Publisher's Cataloging-in-Publication
(Provided by Quality Books, Inc.)

Bell, Laurie Lee.
    Step by step phonics : makes reading and spelling
easy : a comprehensive literacy program for all beginning
readers / Laurie Lee Bell. -- Completely rev. ed.
    p. cm.
    Preassigned LCCN: 98-92893
    ISBN: 0-9643274-8-1
    Includes bibliographical references.

    1. Reading--Phonetic method. 2. English language--
Phonetics. 3. Large type books. I. Title.

LB1050.34.B45 1998   372.46'5
                    QBI98-848

Back to the Basics Publishing
P.O. Box 3055
Rancho Cucamonga, CA 91729
e-mail basicspubl@aol.com

Contents

*This program is dedicated to the future of our children
and the advancement of adult literacy in America.*

*Also, to my daughter, Victoria Nicole Bell,
and my husband, Brian Bell who provided endless hours of patience
during the production of this program.*

*I also thank my parents, Dorothy and Roger Lee, for many years
of attention and support.*

1

Program Overview

After searching many years for an organized, comprehensive, effective, and affordable program on the teaching of reading, I realized it did not exist. Therefore, as a concerned educator and successful first grade teacher, I took it upon myself to develop this program. Teaching someone to read is really quite simple when you have an easy to follow program that works.

When speaking with people about *Step by Step Phonics,* they often ask, "Is it for children or adults?" Both. An adult who cannot read, is just a grown up child who never learned to read in first or second grade. "B" says "b" as in "book" whether you are six or sixty.

During the program the word "students" is used. But whether you are teaching one person to read, or an entire class, you will follow the same process.

This program really puts the reading process into perspective. *First of all, there is a widely accepted myth that: "It is so hard to learn to read."* This is just not true. Finding a reading program which works is the hard part; now you have one.

Second, you need to give the students the proper mindset. When you are teaching someone to read, keep the attitude of: *Reading is easy. You will learn to read.* That is what I always told my students. They expected to learn to read and did just that. *When individuals believe in their ability to succeed, they can succeed.*

The program begins by teaching the basics, the sounds of letters and letter combinations. Then students will learn to read and spell the words in the 40 reading units. Each unit contains five words which follow a particular phonics pattern and five sight words. The words are those which beginning readers and writers need to know as they are frequently used.

Each word in the program is used in the context of a sentence. The sentences start out with easy words so students will gain early reading confidence. Students must learn to read the practice sentences, poems, and ten words in each unit. Each poem is original and reinforces the phonics pattern while providing extra reading practice.

Step by Step Phonics is designed to be easy to follow. Each lesson builds on the previous one. If this program is being used with one person, each lesson may be learned in several days or one week. If you are a teacher, spend one week on each unit.

An important feature of Step by Step Phonics is the way it teaches writing and spelling, in addition to reading. To be successful in life one must have good writing skills. Students need to learn the importance of being able to write. One way to do this is by having them write for practical reasons such as a party invitation or a thank you letter. *Children need to understand that being a good reader and writer is not a choice, but a must.*

In recent years, the educational theory called "whole language" virtually eliminated effective, sequential phonics and sight word instruction. Not encompassing the teaching of the alphabetical principle or phonics in a systematic way is a major weakness in the whole language philosophy. *Step by Step Phonics* ensures students will receive phonics instruction in a structured, systematic way, allowing them to break the alphabetic coding system and learn to read.

It was the rapid reading and writing progress my students made each year, that made me realize my program must be shared with parents, literacy tutors, and other teachers who want an effective reading program for their students. Learning the phonics, spelling patterns, and sight words in this program gives students the solid reading and writing foundation they need.

As you use this program, I readily welcome any questions or comments you may have. You may contact me through Back to the Basics Publishing. The address is on the copyright page. I will look forward to hearing from you!

Author,

Laurie Lee Bell

2

Eight Guidelines for Total Reading Success

1) Be patient.

Give the students ample time to practice reading and spelling the words in each unit. More practice means greater retention while expediting reading progress. Some students will require more practice than others. *It is important to be patient as each student learns at a different pace.*

2) Teach the students a variety of strategies to help with comprehension.

A) Have a thorough understanding of phonics.

In the past, teachers who did teach phonics were criticized that the beginning reader put so much attention on the decoding task that there was a loss in comprehension. That is because the beginning reader should have learned, through systematic phonics instruction, letter sounds and how to put them together automatically.

Once a student is able to instantly recognize letter sounds, phonics patterns, plus the sight words in this program, reading comprehension will excel greatly. *Step by Step Phonics* teaches students to look for patterns and quickly recognize words, making reading for understanding much easier because they can focus on the content and not struggle with the words.

B) I reread what I did not understand.
C) I pictured the story in my head as I read.
D) I made predictions before reading.
E) I can ask for an explanation on a part I do not understand.
F) Periodically, I should pause to summarize my thoughts.

I should ask myself, "What is the main idea?" Students should learn to automatically read the passage over if uncertain about the events in the story.

G) Read to learn specific information.

Books provide a wealth of information. Students must be taught how to use books to learn new information on their own. Older students can teach themselves many things simply by reading including: how to use a computer, improve their study skills, or improve in sports. Once students realize the extensive amount of knowledge available in books, a whole new world of possibilities opens up for them.

H) Allow students to choose some of the titles.

When students are very interested in what they are reading, the comprehension will come more naturally.

3) Teach reading strategies in addition to phonics.

This program primarily teaches phonics; the sounds of letters and letter combinations, referred to as patterns, and commonly used sight words. *Phonics and sight word instruction is the foundation of a successful reading program.* However, using other reading strategies simultaneously will aid in reading ability as the students read books. Students must be taught these strategies.

A) Use the context in these ways:
1) Skip the unknown word, read the rest of the sentence, then go back to it.
2) Break the word into parts to see if part of it is familiar. Example: ed/u/ca/tion
3) Use the words before and after the unknown word to discover the meaning.

B) Look at the pictures for clues.

4) Have students focus on gaining meaning from the text.*

A particular student may read, "The boy went to his *home* to get his cap." (instead of) "The boy went to his *house* to get his cap." Meaning would still be obtained, so substituting home for house would be acceptable, for a beginning reader.

If you correct beginning readers on *every* word, they may become frustrated and want to give up. As students progress through the reading units in this program, their reading accuracy will come along steadily. Because the practice sentences start out with easy to read words, students should be able to read them accurately.

*If the book is being read to learn specific information, such as a nonfiction title, then it is important to read with 100% accuracy.

5) Have a variety of interesting books.

Students will learn to read simply by practicing the sentences and poems in this program along with their phonics and sight word knowledge. To inspire further reading, you may want to have other books available. For instance:

A) Use an "ABC" book to review the letter sounds.
Choose a book that teaches the short vowel sounds as students should learn these first.

B) Read rhyming books.
Allow students to fill in the "missing" rhyming word.

C) Read books with predictable or repeating patterns.
Brown Bear, Brown Bear, What Do You See? by Bill Martin is a very popular book with young children. Because the repeating pattern is easy for children to read, it helps them gain early reading confidence.

D) Have picture books available.
Illustrations should correspond to the words on the page. If you are teaching adults to read, explain that it does not matter that they are learning to read from picture books. We all learned to read this way. Emphasize the most important thing: Soon they will independently be able to read anything they desire!

E) Read to your students.
To teach students about the pleasure in reading, they need to hear entertaining and interesting stories. By realizing that reading can be fun, students will be more motivated to want to learn to read on their own.

F) Make your own read along books.
Use books you already have and tape the words. This gives students the opportunity to practice reading independently and aids in word recognition.

G) Take the students to a library or your local bookstore.
Our goal of creating lifelong readers can only be accomplished by getting beginning readers excited about books. Therefore, students must be given the opportunity to find books they love!

6) During oral reading, do not assist too much!

A) Give students time to figure out what an unknown word is before you help.

B) Encourage students to look for familiar patterns.

For example, if a student was stuck on the word "feel," you should ask what the pattern is, "ee says long e." The student needs to recall previously learned information from the program.

C) When reading with students, point to each word, to teach word recognition and one to one word correspondence.

If students still cannot figure out the word by using their phonics and sight word knowledge, the context of the sentence, or picture clues, you may help. The goal is to have readers make a good attempt to read the words independently before offering assistance.

7) Reading one's own words is a beginning step toward reading books.

A good way to introduce the reading process is by transcribing students' stories. For example, if you spent a day at a museum, have the students describe what happened there and you should write it down. Then have them read it back to you, as you point to each word. Students will be familiar with the written text as it is simply their words on paper. Writing their language makes them understand the connection between speaking, writing, and reading.

After the students have moved through several lessons and understand the basic letter-sound relationships, or phonics, encourage a lot of independent writing. *Do not let the students depend on you.* Make them use what has been learned from this program, about patterns within words and sight words. This is so important in creating an independent writer. Each September I hear, "But I don't know how to write." I respond with, "Write what you can. If you can read it to me, I will accept it. As you go through each reading unit, you will know how to spell a lot more words."

Teachers who tell their students how to spell all the words will create totally dependent writers who never dare write anything by themselves. The rough drafts and early writings will have a lot of errors, accept this. As the students progress through the program and learn to spell more words, writing will improve dramatically. If the students really like a particular writing activity, then you may proofread it and have them write it over error free.

As a child or adult first learns to read and write, it is like breaking a secret code. There is a lot of natural enthusiasm. Therefore, do not insist that every rough draft be written over. This may take the enjoyment out of writing.

8) Do dictation and have students write daily.

This section explains how to use simple dictation to teach students to write conventionally. Dictation means you tell the learner what to write. Whether you are a teacher, parent, or literacy tutor you will follow the same, basic procedure.

Before doing dictation there are some basic writing skills students need to learn. First, they must know how to write the alphabet from memory. Next, they need to know the consonant sounds, ch, ph, sh, th, and wh. Short and long vowel sounds will be covered in the program. They do not need to be thoroughly learned at this time.

Once students have learned these basic sounds, dictate easy sentences to them. Use words that are in the reading unit you are teaching that week, or previously covered reading units. Slowly say each word and really emphasize the sound of each letter, especially the vowels. Here are sample sentences you may say and have them write. *I ran fast. Dad has a hat. The man is tan. I am late for the game.* Writing sentences like these gives students the opportunity to utilize their phonics and sight word knowledge.

After students write each dictated sentence, show them the correct way to write it, on the chalkboard. Have them write the sentence correctly, with pen or colored pencil, below their original attempt. By rewriting each sentence correctly, they learn conventional spelling and sentence structure. Then, have the students read it. Reading the easy sentences will build their confidence as readers. Do simple dictation often as it teaches students to read and write simultaneously.

Spend a lot of time initially teaching students how to write a sentence. Students must be taught to put spaces between words, when to use capitals and lower case letters, and correct punctuation. Once you get students to believe in their ability to read and write, they progress rapidly. Students as young as first grade certainly can learn correct paragraph development. Soon, students will be able to independently write sentences, descriptive paragraphs, and detailed stories. *Your students will rise to your level of expectation. Never underestimate their ability because of their age.*

When teaching students to write sentences, have them focus on improving one skill at a time. For instance, on several lessons have students focus on the need to capitalize at the beginning of the sentence. Once they learn to do this, focus on another skill like correct spacing.

Beginning writers, whether children or adults, are very sensitive to criticism. One harsh critical remark can take away their confidence from their last ten successful accomplishments. If you bombard the beginning writer with all their mistakes, they will feel overwhelmed. Compliment the students on little things they did correctly, even if it was simply remembering to put a space between each word. Children do need to be taught the correct method, but do it tactfully.

Students should have the opportunity to do some type of writing each day. One way to do this is by keeping a journal. Each day students may just want to write about their day, as an adult would in a private diary. To motivate them to write, you could tell them a funny or interesting story that happened to you.

I shared this story with my class. This weekend I went out for breakfast with my husband. I took a sip of coffee and felt something strange in my mouth. I spit out the coffee and foreign object into my napkin. It was a fly! Its wings were dripping wet. It had fallen into my coffee. That was the end of my breakfast!

Sharing your personal stories can motivate students to share their ideas, then write about them. Sometimes I write in my journal while the students are writing. When students see their teacher writing it gives them the message that writing is important. At the end of journal writing, have some of the students read their entries to the class. Having students share what they wrote builds their confidence as they begin to view themselves as readers and writers.

When students write in a journal, it is very easy for them to read the entry because everything is in their own words. Certainly there is a lot of natural, built in comprehension, since they wrote it!

Here are some journal topics for students to choose from:

1. If I was the principal...
2. My dream vacation would be...
3. I am thankful for...
4. My favorite animal...
5. Depending on the time of year give students a sentence starter such as: Christmas is... Spring is... Easter is...
6. A day with no rules...
7. If I had magic powers...
8. My best birthday memory...

9. I wish my parents would...
10. Describe the perfect teacher...
11. If I had a money tree...
12. My favorite subject is...
13. List a food for every letter of the alphabet...
14. I am really proud of myself for...
15. I would like to learn...

It is important to write back to the students in their journals as often as time permits. This really motivates them to want to read as they will want to know what you wrote. Also, they will feel important because of the extra time you took to write to them. Giving students a little extra time and attention will help build their confidence. Whether you are a teacher, parent, or literacy tutor, remember students will achieve more when you can get them to believe in themselves.

By writing back to the students in their journals, you are really teaching them the real meaning of the writing process, which is to communicate. If students love to get personal comments in their journals from a teacher, just think how much they would value a personal comment from a parent who is using this program!

Another way to motivate them to write is by showing them how writing can accomplish many things. For instance, a parent could ask the beginning reader to describe a favorite restaurant and write reasons why they should go there for dinner. Have the student read the journal entry and you could say, "Let's go there tonight!"

If teachers use this program, they should have the students write monthly job application letters for the classroom job of their choice. This would quickly teach students how important it is to be able to communicate effectively. If they want a special job like helper or line leader, they must have a well written letter. *Writing job letters on the first of each month, and displaying them all year long, is a great way to show each student's progress.*

As a teacher, I often read exciting books to motivate the students to write. Read Chapter 8, *Choosing Quality Literature,* for many writing activities to use with books. The more interesting you make the writing topics, the more motivated the students will be to write.

There are many fun and challenging writing activities to do which allow students to practice their writing skills. *Always demonstrate a model lesson first so students know what is expected of them.* Ideas include: ads, advice columns, announcements, autobiographies, beauty tips, campaign speeches, cartoons, descriptions, directions, epitaphs, exaggerations, fables, fairy tales, fashion articles, game rules, greeting cards, grocery lists, interviews, invitations, jokes, jump rope rhymes, letters, lists, monologues, movie reviews or scripts, mysteries, myths, newspapers, opinions, party tips, persuasive letters, plays, poems, ransom notes, resumes, songs, speeches, story, tv commercials, thank you notes, travel posters, want ads, wanted posters, wills, wishes, and weather reports.

Sometimes the students may have a really good writing idea they want to "publish" or do over neatly. It is important to have supplies such as construction paper, glue, crayons, markers, colored pencils, and scissors available. When learning is fun, it keeps students interested and motivated. The goal is to create individuals who want to learn and enjoy doing so!

3

Learn the Consonants and Vowels

Students should be able to write the alphabet from memory plus know which letters are consonants and which are vowels before beginning Reading Unit One.

Consonants: Bb Cc Dd Ff Gg Hh Jj Kk Ll Mm Nn Pp Qq Rr Ss Tt Vv Ww Xx Yy Zz

Vowels: Aa Ee Ii Oo Uu

Point to each letter below and have the students tell you whether it is a consonant or vowel. The easiest way for students to learn this is to remember that the vowels are: **Aa, Ee, Ii, Oo, and Uu.** Therefore, all the other letters must be consonants. This must be learned thoroughly as it will be used to recognize patterns throughout the program. Teachers should write the letters on sentence strips to help the students learn them. *Display a chart with consonants on one side, vowels on the other, for students to refer to.*

G j X U f C l m J E S b P O A M d c R h g

K c L Z N o I Y D p Q i B C e k n V K b a

X W R H w A F s q v I r y Z e i O T J M P

Now the students are ready to learn the sounds on pages 16 and 17. At the beginning of the school year, teachers should photocopy these two pages for homework. Instruct the students to keep the pages at home and learn the sounds. These basic sounds should also be taught in class.

Once students know these sounds, you may photocopy and give them the award on page 204. Throughout the program, it is important to acknowledge each student's progress.

Learn These Sounds

Bb book 	Cc computer
Dd disk	Ff folder
Gg gift	Hh house
Jj jet	Kk key
Ll letter	Mm mailbox
Nn night	Pp pencil

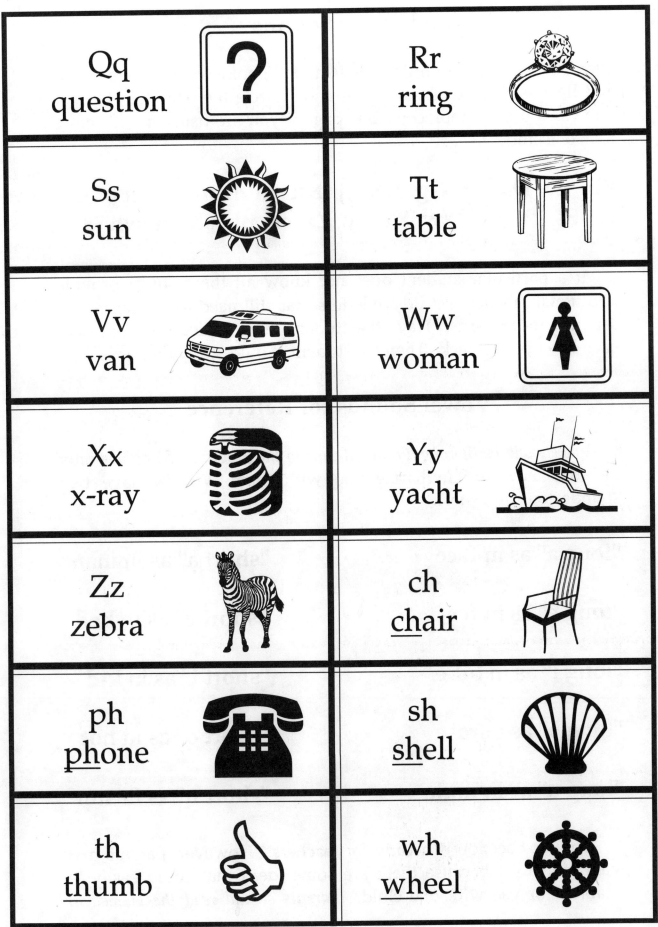

Qq question	Rr ring
Ss sun	Tt table
Vv van	Ww woman
Xx x-ray	Yy yacht
Zz zebra	ch chair
ph phone	sh shell
th thumb	wh wheel

Say the Sounds

Directions: After learning pages 16 and 17, point to the letters below and have each student say the sound. Circle the ones they do not know. You may photocopy this page if you are using it with more than one student.

Bb Cc Dd Ff Gg Hh Jj Kk Ll Mm Nn Pp Qq Rr Ss Tt Vv Ww Xx Yy Zz ch ph sh th wh

If a particular student does not know all the sounds, provide additional practice. Write the letters that still need to be learned on separate index cards. Have the student draw a picure to represent each letter on the back. Then the student should study the cards.

Vowel Sounds for Reference

Vowels will be thoroughly taught during the program. They are only included now to familiarize you with them. Vowels have two sounds, long and short.

"long a" as in **face**	"short a" as in **man**
"long e" as in **feet**	"short e" as in **bed**
"long i" as in **bike**	"short i" as in **kid**
"long o" as in **rose**	"short o" as in **hot**
"long u" as in **mule**	"short u" as in **sun**

The next section is mainly for teachers. However, parents may want to read it because there are some ideas that could easily be adapted for use with one child. *Parents should read the Homework*

Information sheet on page 22. This page explains a good system for helping their child learn the recommended one reading unit per week.

Specific Suggestions for Teachers

All students need to be taught these 31 sounds immediately: the consonant sounds, short vowels, plus the digraphs ch, ph, sh, th, and wh. Teach the hard sound for the letters "c" and "g." This is the sound of "c" as in cat; "g" as in girl. Following is a very effective way for teaching one sound per day at the beginning of the school year, especially for kindergarten and first grade students.

For homework, have students bring an object to school each day which represents a particular sound. On the first day of school, send home a list and schedule for the letters Aa>Zz, ch, ph, sh, th, and wh. Explain that students need to know these sounds and will bring one item each day to represent the letter's sound.

Instruct the parents to keep the schedule of letters and dates on their refrigerator. Tell them you will pick one item each day to display above the alphabet letter or digraph at the front of the room. Items will be returned at the end of the year.

Each day as students show their items, write them on a chart, and practice reading them. On day one, students would share the "short a" items. As you point to the "Aa" wall card, have them say its sound. Choose one item to hang above the wall card for that sound. One year, I had a toy alligator hanging above my "Aa" wall card. Finish the lesson with handwriting practice for "Aa."

The second day, go over the items the students brought for "Bb." Again, list them and review the sounds for "Aa" and "Bb." Then do handwriting practice for "Bb." Continue to do this until the end of the 31 days. On the thirty first day, point to each letter Aa>Zz, ch, ph, sh, th, and wh. Students will tell you each sound.

Sample dialogue: You'll say, "A says, (pause), b says, (pause), c says, (pause...) and continue this method for the entire alphabet. You will pause after each sound so students can tell you the correct sound for each letter or digraph. Continue to review these sounds every day, all year, so new students learn them too. By having real objects displayed above the "ABC" letters, students will readily learn their basic sounds and enjoy doing so.

Following is a strategy to ensure you review the sounds each day. Do it right before handwriting practice. Have students do their handwriting practice in individual alphabet books, which you may staple together from school paper. Students should do several rows of the capital and lower case letter. Then, use the letter in a sentence which represents its sound. Example: "Aa" is for apple. Have students draw a picture to go with the letter.

Homework Information Sheet

Step by Step Phonics should be taught in class and used as part of your homework program for the entire school year. A sample Homework Information sheet is provided on page 22. Staple the Homework Information sheet into a folder. Send the folder home each Monday, with the weekly reading unit, practice sentences, and poem in it. The Homework Information sheet explains to the parents how they will use *Step by Step Phonics* with their child. Have the students return their folder, with their completed work in it, each Friday.

On Friday, give the students a spelling test for that week's reading unit. You should give the students a practice test, the first time, as many will not know how to take a spelling test. For first grade students, I have called it a "perfect test," if they can spell five or more words correctly. Depending on the amount of parental support in your area, you could set a different goal. Some students will have perfect tests all year. Such students will have phenomenal reading and writing ability for their age.

Create a large bulletin board to encourage spelling effort. Take a picture of the students. As they receive perfect scores on their tests, add stars above their pictures. By the end of the year, the students will have many stars displayed, a great way to encourage them to study and master this program. If you prefer, simply make a chart on which you can add stickers for each perfect test.

If several students have a difficult time spelling all the words in each unit correctly, decide on a fair goal for them, so they too can succeed and earn "spelling stars." Perhaps learning to spell the five phonics pattern words could be called a "perfect test," if this was absolutely their best effort. Constantly challenge these students to try to learn to read and spell all the words though.

An excellent homework strategy mentioned on the Homework Information sheet is to have the students learn to read one poem a week and draw a picture to go with it. Students who already know how to read can memorize each week's poem, which will challenge them. Keep all poems until the end of the school year. Then, make individual poem books for the students to keep.

To have students practice reading the weekly poem in class, write it on 12" x 18" white construction paper. Draw a 1" border for each poem's picture. Each week pick a different student to illustrate it. Then, laminate each poem. By the end of your first year of using *Step by Step Phonics*, you will have a laminated copy of each poem. You could bind the enlarged poems with rings and have the whole set ready for use the next year.

Each week, have students spend about five minutes a day reading the poem together. Reinforce how to use the context of the sentence to figure out unknown words in the poem. To help their comprehension, have them tell you what the poem is about.

On Friday, have each student read the poem to you. While individual students come up and read the poem, the rest of the class can work on an independent activity. You should have a special poem award chart to encourage students. Give students a sticker to add each week if they read the poem.

Throughout the year, give awards for the number of poems read and perfect spelling tests. On pages 202 and 203, you will find an end of the year award for total number of poems read plus perfect spelling tests. Always make the students feel important for their accomplishments.

HOMEWORK INFORMATION

Three Reading/Spelling Plans: The goal is to have your child read and spell all ten words in each reading unit. If your child is not ready for Plan Three, begin with Plan One and challenge him/her to progress to Plan Three. The units are from *Step by Step Phonics*, a program carefully designed to teach reading and spelling.

Plan One: Learn the phonics pattern. Learn to <u>read</u> all ten words.
Plan Two: Learn to <u>read and spell</u> the five phonics pattern words. Learn to <u>read</u> the five sight words.
Plan Three: Learn to <u>read and spell</u> all ten words.

<u>Monday</u>: Learn the weekly phonics pattern. Write the phonics pattern words three times each. Use each one in a sentence.
<u>Tuesday</u>: Write the sight words three times each. Use each one in a sentence.
<u>Wednesday</u>: Review the weekly phonics pattern. List as many words as you can that follow the same pattern. Then, practice reading them.
<u>Thursday</u>: Give your child a practice test. Study the incorrect words.
<u>Friday</u>: Spelling test at school. <u>Return all homework in the folder.</u>

Poem: Learn to read it. Draw a picture to go with it. Students who already know how to read should memorize each poem to provide a challenge and strengthen their memory. Poems must be returned on Friday in the homework folder. At the end of the year the poems will be made into a special poem book for your child to keep.

Additional Reading Practice: Spend 15 minutes each night reading with your child. Help your child sound out the words. Encourage your child to look for phonics patterns, recognize sight words, and use the context of the sentence to figure out unknown words. Be patient, learning to read takes time and effort.

Other: Other homework may be in the folder depending on what additional practice students need.

4

Three Individualized Reading Plans

There are three ways of using this program for each unit, all create readers:

Plan One: Learn the phonics pattern. Learn to <u>read</u> all ten words.

Plan Two: Learn to <u>read and spell</u> the five phonics pattern words. Learn to <u>read</u> the five sight words.

Plan Three: Learn to <u>read and spell</u> all ten words.

To develop this program, I analyzed which words students often encounter in their reading, use in their daily language, and have the most difficulty with when spelling. In addition, many accredited word lists were cross referenced before deciding on the placement of the words: Dolch, Fry, Kucera-Francis Corpus, Heath-240 Most Commonly Used, The High Utility 500 by Rebecca Sitton. (Sitton's list was compiled initially from the American Heritage Frequency Study. These words were cross-checked with other respected studies: Gates, Horn, Rinsland, Green, Loomer, Harris, and Johnson.)

Many of the words were able to be grouped by phonics patterns. Those which did not fit any particular pattern were grouped as sight words. Each reading unit contains five words which follow one phonics pattern and five sight words. Frequently used sight words are included in each unit because students will come across them in their reading and they can not be phonetically sounded out. Therefore, students must simply memorize them.

The program teaches words which progress from simple to more complex as the student is ready to learn them. Students should learn one reading unit per week. Have students write sentences for the words in each reading unit. *If a word in the unit is a homonym, make certain the students understand its exact meaning.* For instance, in Reading Unit Three, point out "one" refers to the number.

The goal for each reading unit is to learn and be able to recognize the phonics pattern. During each unit, brainstorm with the students other words which follow the same pattern. For example, Reading Unit One teaches this pattern: Consonant-vowel-consonant words will have the "short a" sound. The words in Unit One are: can, had, has, man, and ran. Once the students learn this phonics pattern they will be able to read and spell many other words which have the same pattern such as: dad, mad, pad, sad, bag, rag, sag, ham, jam, fan, pan, tan, van, cap, lap, nap, tap, bat, cat, hat, mat, and rat.

By learning the 40 patterns in the reading units, individuals will be able to read and spell thousands of words, before the completion of this program. Often a student catches on to the reading process before the tenth unit and becomes an independent reader! However, students who learn to read quickly should finish the program to improve their spelling and writing ability.

Being a good reader, writer, and speller does have a considerable impact on an individual's success in school and in the job market. Therefore, it would be best if the students did Plan Three; learning to read and spell all ten words in each unit. The best readers and writers in your class will be those individuals who do Plan Three. By the end of *Step by Step Phonics*, students will have a solid reading and writing foundation which will give them the confidence and ability they need to succeed in life.

The information in this program is a summary of a great deal of research, effective teaching strategies learned at the university level, countless teaching workshops attended, and what actually worked in my classroom. I could have elaborated endlessly. However, my goal was to keep it simple, easy to use, yet include everything you need to know for total reading success.

5

Implementing the Reading Units

Parents should read this section to get additional ideas for using the program but your child may progress at an individualized pace, not necessarily the suggested one reading unit per week. Allow your child enough time to learn to read and spell all the words before proceeding to the next unit.

If you are a teacher using this program, spend one week on each unit. Use 3 x 24 inch sentence strips, available at school supply stores, to help the class learn each reading unit. Write the phonics pattern and the five words following the pattern on the front of the sentence strip. Write the five sight words on the back. Use Crayola Classic markers as they do not bleed through the sentence strip. See the illustrations below. You may choose to laminate the strips.

Reading Unit 1 (front) Phonics pattern: Consonant-vowel-consonant words will have the "short a" sound. can had has man ran	Reading Unit 1 (back) Sight Words a and is the to

Each Monday, introduce the phonics pattern. Encourage the students to discover the pattern. Have the students read and spell the words. For each week's reading unit, have your students think of other words which follow the same pattern. For example, Reading Unit One teaches "short a." The words are: can, had, has, man, and ran. Challenge students to think of other "short a" words. List these words and have the students practice reading and spelling them. This will help them internalize the patterns and recognize them later when reading.

Once your students can read the phonics pattern words, have them learn to read the phonics pattern sentences. Write the sentences from each unit on chart paper or the chalkboard so the class can practice reading them. Show your students how to use the context of the sentence to figure out the words. If you choose to write the sentences on chart paper, save them for use the following year.

After the students have practiced reading the phonics pattern sentences, have them write the words three times each. Then, they should use each word in a new sentence of their own. Show them how to sound out words. Teach proper sentence structure such as using capital letters, spacing, and correct punctuation. Write the first two sentences as a class. Then, challenge them to write the last three sentences by themselves.

If you have individual chalkboards, this is a convenient way to have students practice spelling the words and writing the sentences. Otherwise, school paper works fine. Repeat the above method for the sight words on Tuesday morning. Do this for each reading unit throughout the year.

In addition to having the students write the phonics pattern words on Monday and the sight words on Tuesday, do the following. On Wednesday, have students practice spelling the phonics pattern words again. On Thursday, have students practice the sight words again. After spelling the sight words on Thursday, give the students a pretest. It is best if you correct them. Pretests help students know which words they still need to learn for Friday's spelling test.

Before you give the spelling test on Friday, have students write all ten spelling words in their individual wordbooks. These are personal dictionaries students can refer to at any time. One year, I displayed all the words from the program on the wall. However, I found students just didn't look at the wall to find the correct spelling of a word from the program. But students do enjoy looking up the *Step by Step Phonics* words in their individual wordbooks as it makes them feel very grown up. Plus, this is also a step toward teaching them independence and research skills.

The more students practice the words, the more retention they will have. You should use the sentence strips to review previously covered reading units throughout the year. Also, if any parents don't follow through on the weekly homework, teaching *Step by Step Phonics* in your class meets the needs for those children.

As you use *Step by Step Phonics*, be patient and encouraging as learning to read will happen at a different pace for each student. The children need you more than you may realize. You may be the only person that can give a particular child the gift of literacy.

6

Reading Units One Through Forty

C=Consonant
V=Vowel

Reading Unit 1

The left column has words which follow a phonics pattern.
The right column has sight words which must be memorized.

**Phonics Pattern: Consonant-vowel-consonant words will
have the "short a" sound.**

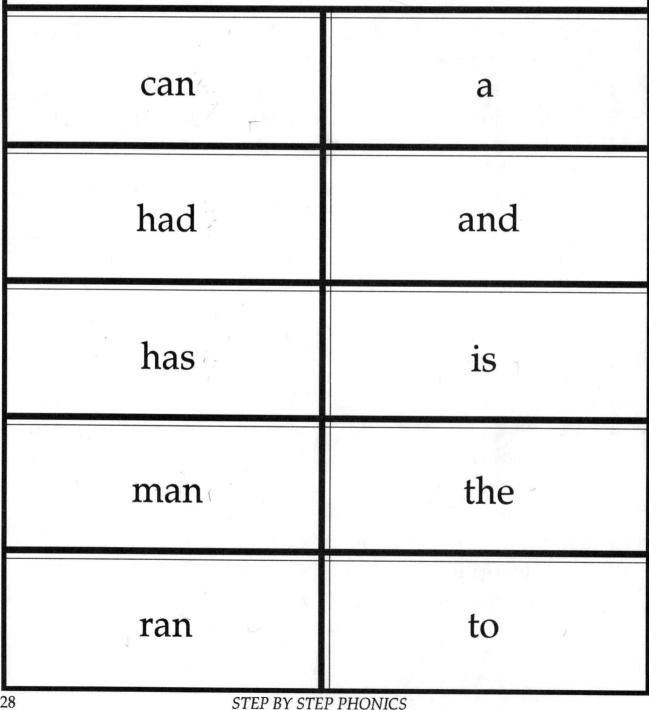

can	a
had	and
has	is
man	the
ran	to

Reading Unit 1

Name_____

Practice reading these sentences.

1. I <u>can</u> do it.

2. Dan <u>had</u> a good day.

3. He <u>has</u> a cat.

4. The <u>man</u> is happy.

5. I <u>ran</u> to see dad.

Write each word three times.

can_____

had_____

has_____

man_____

ran_____

Make up a new sentence for each phonics pattern word.

can_____

had_____

has_____

man_____

ran_____

Reading Unit 1

Name_____

Practice reading these sentences.

1. The man has <u>a</u> tan.
2. Sam <u>and</u> Pat ran fast.
3. He <u>is</u> my friend.
4. <u>The</u> sun is hot.
5. I go <u>to</u> school.

Write each word three times.

a_____

and_____

is_____

the_____

to_____

Make up a new sentence for each sight word. ✶

a_____

and_____

is_____

the_____

to_____

Practice reading this poem.
Draw a picture to go with it.   Name_____

Which Hat?

Blue hat, red hat, yellow hat, green.
Purple hat, orange hat, let me see.
Which hat looks the best on me?
I think you should pick the green.

Reading Unit 2

The left column has words which follow a phonics pattern.
The right column has sight words which must be memorized.

Phonics Pattern: Vowel-consonant words will have the "short a" sound.

ad	in
am	it
an	that
as	was
at	you

Reading Unit 2

Phonics Pattern Words   Name_____

Practice reading these sentences.

1. We put an <u>ad</u> in the paper.
2. I <u>am</u> a good friend.
3. Dad ate <u>an</u> apple.
4. I am <u>as</u> big <u>as</u> Dan.
5. The man is <u>at</u> home.

Write each word three times.

ad_____

am_____

an_____

as_____

at_____

Make up a new sentence for each phonics pattern word.

ad_____

am_____

an_____

as_____

at_____

Reading Unit 2

<u>Sight Words</u>   Name_____

Practice reading these sentences.

1. I am <u>in</u> my room.
2. Look at <u>it</u> rain.
3. <u>That</u> is a good plan.
4. Dad <u>was</u> late.
5. Did <u>you</u> see my hat?

Write each word three times.

in_____

it_____

that_____

was_____

you_____

Make up a new sentence for each sight word. *

in_____

it_____

that_____

was_____

you_____

STEP BY STEP PHONICS

Practice reading this poem.
Draw a picture to go with it.   Name_____

A or An

Use "a" before a consonant sound.
Use "an" before a vowel sound.
A b̲ear, a c̲at, a d̲og,
An e̲lephant or an o̲wl.

Reading Unit 3

The left column has words which follow a phonics pattern.
The right column has sight words which must be memorized.

Phonics Pattern: Adding a "silent e" to a consonant-vowel-consonant word makes the "a" long.
Examples: can>cane mad>made

came	oh
face	on
gave	one
made	said
take	your

Reading Unit 3

Name_____

Practice reading these sentences.

1. I <u>came</u> to see you.
2. She has a pretty <u>face</u>.
3. Pam <u>gave</u> it to me.
4. I <u>made</u> a cake.
5. <u>Take</u> me to the store.

Write each word three times.

came_____

face_____

gave_____

made_____

take_____

Make up a new sentence for each phonics pattern word.

came_____

face_____

gave_____

made_____

take_____

Reading Unit 3

Name_____

Practice reading these sentences.

1. <u>Oh</u>, I can do it!
2. The cat is <u>on</u> the mat.
3. I had <u>one</u> orange.
4. Mom <u>said</u> I can go.
5. <u>Your</u> dad is nice.

Write each word three times.

oh_____

on_____

one_____

said_____

your_____

Make up a new sentence for each sight word.

oh_____

on_____

one_____

said_____

your_____

Practice reading this poem.
Draw a picture to go with it.   Name_____

The Lake

A lake in the spring is a beautiful thing.
But best of all is a lake in the fall.
The leaves drift on down,
Adding colors all around.

Reading Unit 4

The left column has words which follow a phonics pattern.
The right column has sight words which must be memorized.

Phonics Pattern: The letters "ay" have the "long a" sound.

day	boy
may	girl
play	or
say	put
way	some

STEP BY STEP PHONICS

Reading Unit 4

Name_____

Practice reading these sentences.

1. I had fun all <u>day</u>.

2. <u>May</u> I help you?

3. I like to <u>play</u>.

4. What did you <u>say</u>?

5. I'm on my <u>way</u> to school.

Write each word three times.

day_____

may_____

play_____

say_____

way_____

Make up a new sentence for each phonics pattern word.

day_____

may_____

play_____

say_____

way_____

Reading Unit 4

<u>Sight Words</u>   Name_____

Practice reading these sentences.

1. Brad is a <u>boy</u>.

2. Kate is a <u>girl</u>.

3. I can play with you <u>or</u> Sam.

4. Please <u>put</u> it on the table.

5. I had <u>some</u> friends come over.

Write each word three times.

boy_____

girl_____

or_____

put_____

some_____

Make up a new sentence for each sight word.

boy_____

girl_____

or_____

put_____

some_____

STEP BY STEP PHONICS

Practice reading this poem.
Draw a picture to go with it.   Name_____

My Favorite Day

My favorite day is filled with play,
With friends from near and far away.
Friends are great, I must say.
They add joy to every day.

Reading Unit 5

The left column has words which follow a phonics pattern.
The right column has sight words which must be memorized.

**Phonics Pattern: The letters "ai" say "long a." When two
vowels go walking, the first one does the talking.**

mail	are
paid	from
rain	have
tail	I
train	this

Reading Unit 5

Phonics <u>Pattern Words</u>   Name_____

Practice reading these sentences.

1. Please get the <u>mail</u>.
2. Mom <u>paid</u> all the bills.
3. It may <u>rain</u> today.
4. The dog chased its <u>tail</u>.
5. She rode on a <u>train</u>.

Write each word three times.

mail_____

paid_____

rain_____

tail_____

train_____

Make up a new sentence for each phonics pattern word.

mail_____

paid_____

rain_____

tail_____

train_____

Reading Unit 5

Name_____

Practice reading these sentences.

1. <u>Are</u> you ready to go?
2. The letter is <u>from</u> Chad.
3. I <u>have</u> a cat.
4. May <u>I</u> help you?
5. <u>This</u> is a fun game.

Write each word three times.

are_____

from_____

have_____

I_____

this_____

Make up a new sentence for each sight word.

are_____

from_____

have_____

I_____

this_____

Practice reading this poem.
Draw a picture to go with it.   Name_____

Listen to the Rain

Sprinkle, sprankle, sprinkle, sprankle,
Splish, splash, splish, splash,
Listen to the rain.
Listen to the rain.

Reading Unit 6

The left column has words which follow a phonics pattern.
The right column has sight words which must be memorized.

Phonics Pattern: Consonant-vowel-consonant words will have the "short e" sound.

get	there
let	they
men	use
red	went
yes	when

Reading Unit 6

Name_____

Practice reading these sentences.

1. I may <u>get</u> a pet.
2. Mom <u>let</u> me play in the rain.
3. Some <u>men</u> came to visit dad.
4. <u>Red</u> is my favorite color.
5. <u>Yes</u>, you may play outside.

Write each word three times.

get_____

let_____

men_____

red_____

yes_____

Make up a new sentence for each phonics pattern word.

get_____

let_____

men_____

red_____

yes_____

Reading Unit 6

Name_____

Practice reading these sentences.

1. I may go <u>there</u> today.
2. <u>They</u> are in the car.
3. May I <u>use</u> your train set?
4. Pat and I <u>went</u> to a movie.
5. <u>When</u> will we have lunch?

Write each word three times.

there_____

they_____

use_____

went_____

when_____

Make up a new sentence for each sight word.

there_____

they_____

use_____

went_____

when_____

Practice reading this poem.
Draw a picture to go with it.   Name_____

Covered in Red

"Yes," said the man all covered in red.
"I painted my house and I painted my head.
I'd better stop right now and clean up instead.
I'm tired from so much painting, it's time for bed!"

Reading Unit 7

The left column has words which follow a phonics pattern.
The right column has sight words which must be memorized.

Phonics Pattern: The letter "e" at the end of a one syllable word says "long e."

be	do
he	here
me	if
she	us
we	will

STEP BY STEP PHONICS

Reading Unit 7

Name_____

Practice reading these sentences.

1. Will you <u>be</u> my friend?
2. <u>He</u> went to get the mail.
3. Ted came to visit <u>me</u>.
4. <u>She</u> is fun to play with.
5. <u>We</u> had a lot of work to do.

Write each word three times.

be_____

he_____

me_____

she_____

we_____

Make up a new sentence for each phonics pattern word.

be_____

he_____

me_____

she_____

we_____

Reading Unit 7

Name_____

Practice reading these sentences.

1. I must <u>do</u> my homework.
2. Put the game <u>here</u>.
3. I will ask Dave <u>if</u> he can stay.
4. She came with <u>us</u>.
5. <u>Will</u> you help me?

Write each word three times.

do_____

here_____

if_____

us_____

will_____

Make up a new sentence for each sight word.

do_____

here_____

if_____

us_____

will_____

Practice reading this poem.
Draw a picture to go with it.   Name_____

Look at Me

Look at me, I'm small but smart.
What you can't see is my big, kind heart.
It doesn't matter if you're young or old.
A fine way to be is with a heart of gold.

Reading Unit 8

The left column has words which follow a phonics pattern.
The right column has sight words which must be memorized.

Phonics Pattern: The letters "ee" say "long e."

feel	her
green	of
keep	want
see	who
three	with

STEP BY STEP PHONICS

Reading Unit 8

<u>Phonics Pattern Words</u>   Name_____

Practice reading these sentences.

1. How do you <u>feel</u> today?
2. The rain made the grass <u>green</u>.
3. Will you <u>keep</u> this for me?
4. Did you <u>see</u> the rainbow?
5. The girl is <u>three</u> years old.

Write each word three times.

feel_____

green_____

keep_____

see_____

three_____

Make up a new sentence for each phonics pattern word.

feel_____

green_____

keep_____

see_____

three_____

Reading Unit 8

Name_____

Practice reading these sentences.

1. Ben saw <u>her</u> at the park.
2. Did you get plenty <u>of</u> rest?
3. I <u>want</u> to play a game.
4. Do you know <u>who</u> broke the vase?
5. Jason wants me to go <u>with</u> you.

Write each word three times.

her_____

of_____

want_____

who_____

with_____

Make up a new sentence for each sight word.

her_____

of_____

want_____

who_____

with_____

Practice reading this poem.
Draw a picture to go with it.   Name_____

Time to Sleep

I see it's time once again,
For you to go to sleep.
The day has slowly slipped away,
But the memories you will keep.

Reading Unit 9

The left column has words which follow a phonics pattern. The right column has sight words which must be memorized.

Phonics Pattern: The letters "ea" say "long e." When two vowels go walking, the first one does the talking.

dear	friend
each	give
eat	goes
please	money
read	two

Reading Unit 9

Practice reading these sentences.

1. A letter may begin with <u>dear</u>.

2. <u>Each</u> person is important.

3. What did you <u>eat</u> today?

4. <u>Please</u> talk to me before you leave.

5. *Step by Step Phonics* helps me <u>read</u>!

Write each word three times.

dear_____

each_____

eat_____

please_____

read_____

Make up a new sentence for each phonics pattern word.

dear_____

each_____

eat_____

please_____

read_____

Reading Unit 9

Name_____

Practice reading these sentences.

1. Kate is my best <u>friend</u>.
2. Remember to <u>give</u> me your phone number.
3. She <u>goes</u> to the library every week.
4. Dad gave me some <u>money</u>.
5. I have <u>two</u> new pencils.

Write each word three times.

friend_____

give_____

goes_____

money_____

two_____

Make up a new sentence for each sight word.

friend_____

give_____

goes_____

money_____

two_____

Practice reading this poem.
Draw a picture to go with it.   Name_____

I Can Learn to Read

I can learn to read and
I can learn to write.
I can learn to spell,
If I study my
Step by Step Phonics every night!

Reading Unit 10

The left column has words which follow a phonics pattern.
The right column has sight words which must be memorized.

Phonics Pattern: The letter "y" at the end of a word with two or more syllables says "long e."

any	done
family	for
funny	love
story	saw
very	what

Reading Unit 10

　　　　Name_____

Practice reading these sentences.

1. Do you need <u>any</u> help?
2. I have fun with my <u>family</u>.
3. Did you hear the <u>funny</u> joke?
4. She told me a scary <u>story</u>.
5. I keep my room <u>very</u> clean.

Write each word three times.

any_____

family_____

funny_____

story_____

very_____

Make up a new sentence for each phonics pattern word.

any_____

family_____

funny_____

story_____

very_____

Reading Unit 10

Name_____

Practice reading these sentences.

1. You have <u>done</u> a good job.

2. Grandma will be here <u>for</u> a day.

3. I <u>love</u> reading a good book.

4. We <u>saw</u> elephants at the zoo.

5. <u>What</u> are you doing tonight?

Write each word three times.

done_____

for_____

love_____

saw_____

what_____

Make up a new sentence for each sight word.

done_____

for_____

love_____

saw_____

what_____

Practice reading this poem.
Draw a picture to go with it.   Name_____

Happy

Let me tell you a secret,
Only this one you may tell.
The sure way to be happy,
Is to treat others very well.

Reading Unit 11

The left column has words which follow a phonics pattern.
The right column has sight words which must be memorized.

**Phonics Pattern: Consonant-vowel-consonant words will
have the "short i" sound.**

big	ate
did	because
his	only
sit	tell
six	then

STEP BY STEP PHONICS

Reading Unit 11

Name_____

Practice reading these sentences.

1. Dad made a <u>big</u> lunch for us.

2. <u>Did</u> you do your homework?

3. The boy played with <u>his</u> puppy.

4. Do you want me to <u>sit</u> here?

5. We will leave at <u>six</u> o'clock.

Write each word three times.

big_____

did_____

his_____

sit_____

six_____

Make up a new sentence for each phonics pattern word.

big_____

did_____

his_____

sit_____

six_____

Reading Unit 11

Name_____

Practice reading these sentences.

1. Danny <u>ate</u> a healthy snack.

2. I am late <u>because</u> I got lost.

3. The boy is <u>only</u> six.

4. Will you <u>tell</u> me a story?

5. Make your bed, <u>then</u> you can play.

Write each word three times.

ate_____

because_____

only_____

tell_____

then_____

Make up a new sentence for each sight word.

ate_____

because_____

only_____

tell_____

then_____

Practice reading this poem.
Draw a picture to go with it.   Name_____

Six Years Old

I learned to read at six years old.
My parents were proud of me.
If you're a bit older, just learning to read,
This program will be very helpful indeed!

Reading Unit 12

The left column has words which follow a phonics pattern.
The right column has sight words which must be memorized.

Phonics Pattern: Adding a "silent e" to a consonant-vowel-consonant word makes the "i" long.
Examples: hid>hide Tim>time

five	first
like	him
nice	more
side	other
time	write

Reading Unit 12

Practice reading these sentences.

1. Tim will be <u>five</u> this year.
2. I really <u>like</u> learning to read.
3. My teacher is very <u>nice</u> to us.
4. Please sit by my <u>side</u>.
5. It is <u>time</u> for you to go to bed.

Write each word three times.

five_____

like_____

nice_____

side_____

time_____

Make up a new sentence for each phonics pattern word.

five_____

like_____

nice_____

side_____

time_____

Reading Unit 12

Name_____

Practice reading these sentences.
1. Kim got <u>first</u> place in the race.
2. I went with <u>him</u> to the lake.
3. May I have a little <u>more</u> fruit?
4. Will you bring me the <u>other</u> key?
5. It is polite to <u>write</u> thank you letters.

Write each word three times.

first_____

him_____

more_____

other_____

write_____

Make up a new sentence for each sight word.

first_____

him_____

more_____

other_____

write_____

Practice reading this poem.
Draw a picture to go with it.   Name_____

A Kite

Sometimes I wish that I could be,
Carefree like a kite.
And do anything I'd like,
Any time, day or night!

Reading Unit 13

The left column has words which follow a phonics pattern.
The right column has sight words which must be memorized.

Phonics Pattern: The letter "y" at the end of a one syllable word says "long i."

by	been
fly	great
my	says
try	them
why	these

Reading Unit 13

Name_____

Practice reading these sentences.

1. We walked <u>by</u> the zoo.
2. This year we will <u>fly</u> in a plane.
3. Do you like <u>my</u> new hat?
4. I want you to <u>try</u> your best.
5. <u>Why</u> did you stay up so late?

Write each word three times.

by_____

fly_____

my_____

try_____

why_____

Make up a new sentence for each phonics pattern word.

by_____

fly_____

my_____

try_____

why_____

Reading Unit 13

<u>Sight Words</u>

Practice reading these sentences.

1. We have <u>been</u> busy this week.
2. We had a <u>great</u> time on our vacation.
3. Mom <u>says</u> get your work done.
4. I saw <u>them</u> at the lake.
5. Look at all <u>these</u> pretty roses.

Write each word three times.

been_____

great_____

says_____

them_____

these_____

Make up a new sentence for each sight word.

been_____

great_____

says_____

them_____

these_____

Practice reading this poem.
Draw a picture to go with it.   Name_____

Why Can't I?

Birds can fly and bees can fly.
Even frisbees do.
As I gaze up at the sky,
I wonder, why can't I fly too?

Reading Unit 14

The left column has words which follow a phonics pattern.
The right column has sight words which must be memorized.

Phonics Pattern: With "ght" in a word, the "gh" is silent.

light	color
night	come
right	long
bought	near
thought	over

Reading Unit 14

<u>Phonics Pattern Words</u>   Name_____

Practice reading these sentences.

1. Please turn on the <u>light</u>.

2. Which <u>night</u> can you come over?

3. She got the answer <u>right</u>.

4. We <u>bought</u> a new car.

5. I <u>thought</u> it was time to leave.

Write each word three times.

light_____

night_____

right_____

bought_____

thought_____

Make up a new sentence for each phonics pattern word.

light_____

night_____

right_____

bought_____

thought_____

Reading Unit 14

Name_____

Practice reading these sentences.

1. Green is my favorite <u>color</u>.

2. Would you like to <u>come</u> with me?

3. We had to wait a <u>long</u> time.

4. Do you live <u>near</u> the beach?

5. I'm going <u>over</u> to Bob's house.

Write each word three times.

color_____

come_____

long_____

near_____

over_____

Make up a new sentence for each sight word.

color_____

come_____

long_____

near_____

over_____

Practice reading this poem.
Draw a picture to go with it.   Name_____

Who's Right?

I may be wrong, you may be right.
But one thing is for certain, it's better not to fight.
Whenever people fight, no one really wins,
They might even lose a very special friend.

Reading Unit 15

The left column has words which follow a phonics pattern.
The right column has sight words which must be memorized.

Phonics Pattern: Consonant-vowel-consonant words will have the "short o" sound.
Contractions should be taught during this unit.

box	can't
dog	didn't
hot	don't
not	I'm
top	you're

STEP BY STEP PHONICS

Reading Unit 15

<u>Phonics Pattern Words</u>   Name_____

Practice reading these sentences.

1. What is in the <u>box</u>?

2. Did you feed the <u>dog</u>?

3. It is very <u>hot</u> outside.

4. I can <u>not</u> find my glasses.

5. That is a pretty <u>top</u> you have on.

Write each word three times.

box_____

dog_____

hot_____

not_____

top_____

Make up a new sentence for each phonics pattern word.

box_____

dog_____

hot_____

not_____

top_____

Reading Unit 15

Practice reading these sentences.

1. I <u>can't</u> lift this heavy box.
2. We <u>didn't</u> have time to shop.
3. Please <u>don't</u> wake up the baby.
4. <u>I'm</u> going to play baseball today.
5. <u>You're</u> a very nice friend.

Write each word three times.

can't_____

didn't_____

don't_____

I'm_____

you're_____

Make up a new sentence for each sight word.

can't_____

didn't_____

don't_____

I'm_____

you're_____

Practice reading this poem.
Draw a picture to go with it.   Name_____

My Dog

I must warn you about my dog.
His favorite thing to do is
Sit by the gate and wait
For his dinner to walk by!

Reading Unit 16

Learn the phonics pattern for the words in the left column. The right column has sight words which must be memorized.

Phonics Pattern: Adding a "silent e" to a consonant-vowel-consonant word makes the "o" long.

Examples: not>note hop>hope

home	after
hope	end
nose	might
note	myself
woke	pretty

STEP BY STEP PHONICS

Reading Unit 16

Phonics Pattern Words

Practice reading these sentences.

1. We live in a nice <u>home</u>.
2. I <u>hope</u> it stops raining soon.
3. My <u>nose</u> is red because of my cold.
4. What did the <u>note</u> say?
5. Mom <u>woke</u> me up very early.

Write each word three times.

home_____

hope_____

nose_____

note_____

woke_____

Make up a new sentence for each phonics pattern word.

home_____

hope_____

nose_____

note_____

woke_____

Reading Unit 16

Name_____

Practice reading these sentences.

1. <u>After</u> school you may have a snack.
2. Kim was at the <u>end</u> of the line.
3. Zack <u>might</u> take a short nap.
4. I read the whole book by <u>myself</u>.
5. That is a very <u>pretty</u> dress.

Write each word three times.

after_____

end_____

might_____

myself_____

pretty_____

Make up a new sentence for each sight word.

after_____

end_____

might_____

myself_____

pretty_____

Practice reading this poem.
Draw a picture to go with it.   Name_____

My Dream Home

I hope someday I'll have a home,
With a beautiful yard and pool.
My teacher says dreams will come true,
With hard work and learning in school.

Reading Unit 17

The left column has words which follow a phonics pattern.
The right column has sight words which must be memorized.

Phonics Pattern: The letters "oa" say "long o." When two vowels go walking, the first one does the talking.

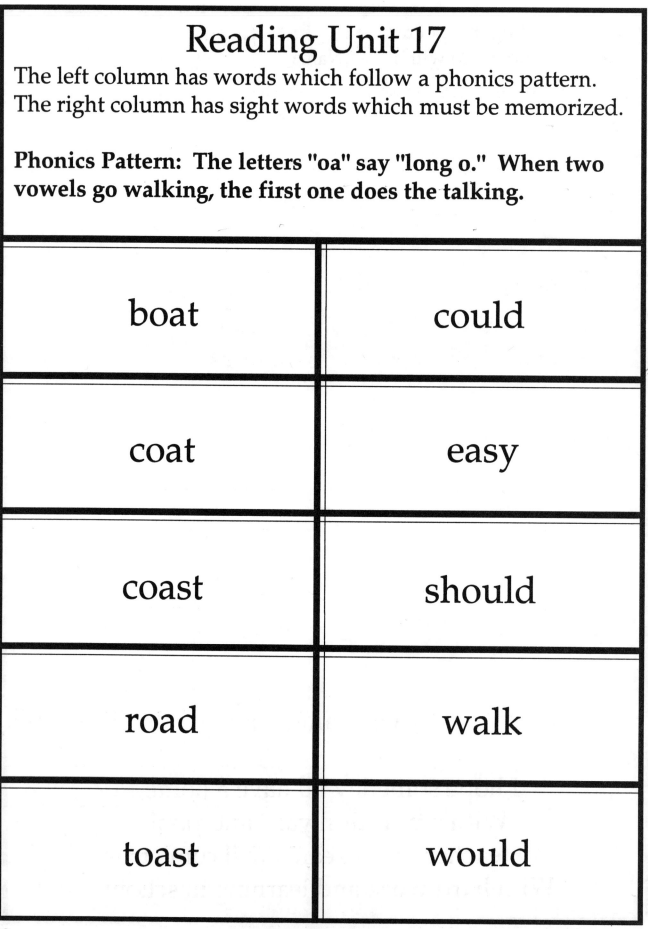

boat	could
coat	easy
coast	should
road	walk
toast	would

STEP BY STEP PHONICS

Reading Unit 17

<u>Phonics Pattern Words</u>   Name_____

Practice reading these sentences.

1. Let's take the <u>boat</u> to the lake.
2. You should bring your <u>coat</u>.
3. It is pretty by the <u>coast</u>.
4. We drove a long way on this <u>road</u>.
5. Would you like <u>toast</u> for breakfast?

Write each word three times.

boat_____

coat_____

coast_____

road_____

toast_____

Make up a new sentence for each phonics pattern word.

boat_____

coat_____

coast_____

road_____

toast_____

Reading Unit 17

<u>Sight Words</u>   Name_____

Practice reading these sentences.

1. <u>Could</u> you two help me?
2. I thought the test was <u>easy</u>.
3. You <u>should</u> make your bed.
4. Danny and I went for a <u>walk</u>.
5. <u>Would</u> you like to go swimming?

Write each word three times.

could_____

easy_____

should_____

walk_____

would_____

Make up a new sentence for each sight word.

could_____

easy_____

should_____

walk_____

would_____

Practice reading this poem.
Draw a picture to go with it.   Name_____

Coast Life

Living on the coast is just fine,
Being on a boat most of the time.
What a great way to spend a summer,
Until Mr. Shark came, what a bummer!

Reading Unit 18

The left column has words which follow a phonics pattern.
The right column has sight words which must be memorized.

Phonics Pattern: The letter "o" at the end of a syllable says "long o."

also	almost
hello	little
go	sure
no	were
so	work

Reading Unit 18

Phonics Pattern Words   Name_____

Practice reading these sentences.

1. You must <u>also</u> make your bed.
2. Mike said <u>hello</u> to me.
3. Would you like to <u>go</u> fishing with me?
4. <u>No</u>, you may not eat that cake.
5. I came home late <u>so</u> I got in trouble.

Write each word three times.

also_____

hello_____

go_____

no_____

so_____

Make up a new sentence for each phonics pattern word.

also_____

hello_____

go_____

no_____

so_____

Reading Unit 18

Name_____

Practice reading these sentences.

1. Are you <u>almost</u> ready to go?
2. The new baby is so <u>little</u>!
3. Kenny is <u>sure</u> he can stay here.
4. Where <u>were</u> you last night?
5. Hard <u>work</u> can make dreams come true.

Write each word three times.

almost_____

little_____

sure_____

were_____

work_____

Make up a new sentence for each sight word.

almost_____

little_____

sure_____

were_____

work_____

Practice reading this poem.
Draw a picture to go with it.   Name_____

Yes, No, Maybe

I say yes, you say no.
I say stop and you say go.
Will we ever agree?
I say hello, you say goodbye.
Getting along, you do need to try.

Reading Unit 19

The left column has words which follow a phonics pattern.
The right column has sight words which must be memorized.

Phonics Pattern: Consonant-vowel-consonant words will have the "short u" sound.

but	early
cut	people
fun	ready
run	think
sun	used

Reading Unit 19

<u>Phonics Pattern Words</u>   Name_____

Practice reading these sentences.

1. I would help you <u>but</u> I'm busy.

2. Please <u>cut</u> on the dotted line.

3. We had a <u>fun</u> time at the museum.

4. Mike likes to <u>run</u> at the beach.

5. The <u>sun</u> is very bright.

Write each word three times.

but_____

cut_____

fun_____

run_____

sun_____

Make up a new sentence for each phonics pattern word.

but_____

cut_____

fun_____

run_____

sun_____

Reading Unit 19

Practice reading these sentences.

1. You need to get up <u>early</u> tomorrow.
2. A lot of <u>people</u> were at the mall.
3. Are you <u>ready</u> for school to start?
4. Do you <u>think</u> you can come over?
5. When I was a baby, I <u>used</u> to cry a lot.

Write each word three times.

early_____

people_____

ready_____

think_____

used_____

Make up a new sentence for each sight word.

early_____

people_____

ready_____

think_____

used_____

Practice reading this poem.
Draw a picture to go with it.   Name_____

Mr. Sun

The darkness slowly fades as
Mr. Sun begins to shine.
The children know the fun will start.
They run and laugh and play.
But then the dark comes again,
Mr. Sun has gone away.

Reading Unit 20

The left column has words which follow a phonics pattern.
The right column has sight words which must be memorized.

Phonics Pattern: Adding a "silent e" to a consonant-vowel-consonant word makes the "u" long.
Examples: cut>cute tub>tube

cute	buy
huge	carry
June	four
rude	lived
rule	once

STEP BY STEP PHONICS

Reading Unit 20

Phonics Pattern Words   Name_____

Practice reading these sentences.

1. The little kitten is so <u>cute</u>.
2. Our neighbor has a <u>huge</u> dog.
3. School is done in <u>June</u>.
4. Do not be <u>rude</u> to others.
5. I think that is a good <u>rule</u>.

Write each word three times.

cute_____

huge_____

June_____

rude_____

rule_____

Make up a new sentence for each phonics pattern word.

cute_____

huge_____

June_____

rude_____

rule_____

Reading Unit 20

Name_____

Practice reading these sentences.

1. What did you <u>buy</u> at the store?
2. I don't think I'm strong enough to <u>carry</u> this.
3. Tonight <u>four</u> of my friends are coming over.
4. My mom <u>lived</u> here since she was little.
5. <u>Once</u> upon a time is how fairy tales begin.

Write each word three times.

buy_____

carry_____

four_____

lived_____

once_____

Make up a new sentence for each sight word.

buy_____

carry_____

four_____

lived_____

once_____

Practice reading this poem.
Draw a picture to go with it.   Name_____

Rules

When I was a child,
I wondered why there were so many rules.
Like, don't put your elbows on the table.
Don't talk to strangers and you must always share.
But now that I'm older I realize parents really care.

Reading Unit 21

The left column has words which follow a phonics pattern.
The right column has sight words which must be memorized.

Phonics Pattern: Learn the two sounds of "ow."

how	live
now	our
grow	remember
know	water
show	where

Reading Unit 21

<u>Phonics Pattern Words</u>   Name_____

Practice reading these sentences.

1. Please tell me <u>how</u> to fix this.
2. I'm almost ready to go <u>now</u>.
3. It is easy to <u>grow</u> pretty flowers.
4. Do you <u>know</u> what time it is?
5. Let me <u>show</u> you how to do it first.

Write each word three times.

how_____

now_____

grow_____

know_____

show_____

Make up a new sentence for each phonics pattern word.

how_____

now_____

grow_____

know_____

show_____

Reading Unit 21

Name_____

Practice reading these sentences.

1. We <u>live</u> in a nice town.
2. Have you been to <u>our</u> home before?
3. Did you <u>remember</u> to bring your keys?
4. You should drink a lot of <u>water</u>.
5. Do you know <u>where</u> I put my watch?

Write each word three times.

live_____

our_____

remember_____

water_____

where_____

Make up a new sentence for each sight word.

live_____

our_____

remember_____

water_____

where_____

Practice reading this poem.
Draw a picture to go with it.   Name_____

When I Grow Up

When I grow up I'll work hard for things,
The kind of things fit for a king.
Beautiful clothes, a castle, diamonds, and rings.
But a loving family is the most important thing!

Reading Unit 22

The left column has words which follow a phonics pattern.
The right column has sight words which must be memorized.

Phonics Pattern: Learn the sound of "ou."

found	about
ground	does
house	strong
out	today
sound	woman

Reading Unit 22

Practice reading these sentences.

1. I <u>found</u> these shoes in the yard.
2. We planted some seeds in the <u>ground</u>.
3. My family bought a new <u>house</u>.
4. Will you carry this <u>out</u> to the car?
5. What was that funny <u>sound</u>?

Write each word three times.

found_____

ground_____

house_____

out_____

sound_____

Make up a new sentence for each phonics pattern word.

found_____

ground_____

house_____

out_____

sound_____

Reading Unit 22

　　　　　Name_____

Practice reading these sentences.

1. You have <u>about</u> ten minutes to get ready.
2. Victoria always <u>does</u> very neat work.
3. Exercising will make your body <u>strong</u>.
4. It looks like <u>today</u> will be sunny.
5. My teacher is a helpful <u>woman</u>.

Write each word three times.

about_____

does_____

strong_____

today_____

woman_____

Make up a new sentence for each sight word.

about_____

does_____

strong_____

today_____

woman_____

Practice reading this poem.
Draw a picture to go with it.   Name_____

Our House

All children need one main thing in their house.
It's not the size, color, or style, I've found.
It's the love within the family that matters,
So they feel cared for, safe, and sound.

Reading Unit 23

The left column has words which follow a phonics pattern.
The right column has sight words which must be memorized.

Phonics Pattern: Learn the two sounds of "oo."

good	another
look	ask
took	even
food	such
soon	those

STEP BY STEP PHONICS

Reading Unit 23

Name_____

Practice reading these sentences.

1. This is a <u>good</u> time to take a break.
2. Go outside and <u>look</u> at the pretty sunset.
3. Who <u>took</u> the book off the shelf?
4. You should always eat healthy <u>food.</u>
5. I hope Uncle Brad comes to visit <u>soon</u>.

Write each word three times.

good_____

look_____

took_____

food_____

soon_____

Make up a new sentence for each phonics pattern word.

good_____

look_____

took_____

food_____

soon_____

Reading Unit 23

<u>Sight Words</u>   Name_____

Practice reading these sentences.

1. It looks like it will be <u>another</u> rainy day.
2. Will you <u>ask</u> Dad if we can go swimming?
3. I do not <u>even</u> know your name.
4. We had <u>such</u> a great time at the lake.
5. Did you see how fast <u>those</u> girls ran?

Write each word three times.

another_____

ask_____

even_____

such_____

those_____

Make up a new sentence for each sight word.

another_____

ask_____

even_____

such_____

those_____

Practice reading this poem.
Draw a picture to go with it.　　Name_____

Food Groups

Milk group, meat group, good to eat.
Bread and cereal, can't be beat.
Fruits and vegetables, eat, eat eat!
To stay healthy, skip the sweets.

Reading Unit 24

The left column has words which follow a phonics pattern.
The right column has sight words which must be memorized.

Phonics Pattern: Learn the sound of "ar."

car	really
dark	school
hard	spell
large	truly
start	year

Reading Unit 24

Practice reading these sentences.

1. What is your favorite kind of <u>car</u>?

2. When I was young, I was afraid of the <u>dark</u>.

3. Do you think these reading units are <u>hard</u>?

4. We plant a <u>large</u> garden every spring.

5. The race will <u>start</u> early in the morning.

Write each word three times.

car_____

dark_____

hard_____

large_____

start_____

Make up a new sentence for each phonics pattern word.

car_____

dark_____

hard_____

large_____

start_____

Reading Unit 24

Name_____

Practice reading these sentences.

1. Did you <u>really</u> want to go the beach today?
2. What do you like best about <u>school</u>?
3. *Step by Step Phonics* teaches you to <u>spell</u>.
4. I <u>truly</u> enjoyed seeing you again.
5. This <u>year</u> has gone so quickly.

Write each word three times.

really_____

school_____

spell_____

truly_____

year_____

Make up a new sentence for each sight word.

really_____

school_____

spell_____

truly_____

year_____

Practice reading this poem.
Draw a picture to go with it.   Name_____

Wish Upon a Star

I often wish upon a star,
To find out dear friend, where you are.
You left my side so long ago,
Will you ever return?
I do hope so.

Reading Unit 25

The left column has words which follow a phonics pattern.
The right column has sight words which must be memorized.

Phonics Pattern: Adding a "silent e" to "ar" changes its sound.
Examples: car>care star>stare

care	different
dare	door
rare	too
square	their
stare	which

STEP BY STEP PHONICS

Reading Unit 25

<u>Phonics Pattern Words</u>　　　　Name_____

Practice reading these sentences.

1. Do you <u>care</u> if I play with your game?
2. I do not <u>dare</u> go on that scary ride.
3. It is very <u>rare</u> to find money.
4. A <u>square</u> has four equal sides.
5. People say it is rude to <u>stare</u>.

Write each word three times.

care_____

dare_____

rare_____

square_____

stare_____

Make up a new sentence for each phonics pattern word.

care_____

dare_____

rare_____

square_____

stare_____

Reading Unit 25

Name_____

Practice reading these sentences.

1. We drove home a <u>different</u> way.
2. When you go outside, close the <u>door</u>.
3. Please don't be gone <u>too</u> long.
4. I just love <u>their</u> new home.
5. Did you see <u>which</u> way the car went?

Write each word three times.

different_____

door_____

too_____

their_____

which_____

Make up a new sentence for each sight word.

different_____

door_____

too_____

their_____

which_____

Practice reading this poem.
Draw a picture to go with it.   Name_____

Please Don't Stare

When you go to the zoo, it's always fun to stare,
At all the fine creatures who make their home there.
But was I ever shocked when I heard,
"Please don't stare."
I looked all around and only saw a bear!

Reading Unit 26

The left column has words which follow a phonics pattern.
The right column has sight words which must be memorized.

Phonics Pattern: Learn the sound of "or."

before	eight
horse	finally
morning	idea
short	number
store	warm

STEP BY STEP PHONICS

Reading Unit 26

<u>Phonics Pattern Words</u>   Name_____

Practice reading these sentences.

1. We need to leave <u>before</u> it gets dark.

2. My friend has a <u>horse</u> on his farm.

3. What time do you get up in the <u>morning</u>?

4. The boy is too <u>short</u> to go on the ride.

5. We'll go to the <u>store</u> when Nikki gets home.

Write each word three times.

before_____

horse_____

morning_____

short_____

store_____

Make up a new sentence for each phonics pattern word.

before_____

horse_____

morning_____

short_____

store_____

Reading Unit 26

Practice reading these sentences.

1. A stop sign has <u>eight</u> sides.
2. I am glad summer is <u>finally</u> here.
3. Going to the zoo is a good <u>idea</u>.
4. There are a <u>number</u> of things to do at camp.
5. Your new coat looks really <u>warm</u>.

Write each word three times.

eight_____

finally_____

idea_____

number_____

warm_____

Make up a new sentence for each sight word.

eight_____

finally_____

idea_____

number_____

warm_____

Practice reading this poem.
Draw a picture to go with it.   Name_____

Morning

Everything is so peaceful and quiet,
In the early morning hours,
Before the busy day begins.
A quiet, relaxing morning
Is the best way to start the day.

Reading Unit 27

The left column has words which follow a phonics pattern.
The right column has sight words which must be memorized.

Phonics Pattern: Learn the sound of "all."

ball	beautiful
called	change
fall	kind
small	move
tall	sentence

STEP BY STEP PHONICS

Reading Unit 27

<u>Phonics Pattern Words</u>   Name_____

Practice reading these sentences.

1. What color <u>ball</u> did you buy?
2. Mom <u>called</u> to say she would be late.
3. Be careful or you may <u>fall</u> down.
4. I wonder what is in that <u>small</u> present.
5. Brandon may be <u>tall</u> when he grows up.

Write each word three times.

ball_____

called_____

fall_____

small_____

tall_____

Make up a new sentence for each phonics pattern word.

ball_____

called_____

fall_____

small_____

tall_____

Reading Unit 27

Name_____

Practice reading these sentences.

1. The bride wore a <u>beautiful</u> wedding dress.
2. How much <u>change</u> will I get back from my dollar?
3. It is a good idea to be <u>kind</u> to others.
4. We will <u>move</u> into a new home in March.
5. By now, I'm sure you can easily write a <u>sentence</u>!

Write each word three times.

beautiful_____

change_____

kind_____

move_____

sentence_____

Make up a new sentence for each sight word.

beautiful_____

change_____

kind_____

move_____

sentence_____

Practice reading this poem.
Draw a picture to go with it.   Name_____

Growing Up

Last year when I was small,
I could not read a book.
This fall I learned my phonics,
I'm reading, take a look!

Reading Unit 28

The left column has words which follow a phonics pattern.
The right column has sight words which must be memorized.

Phonics Pattern: Learn the sound of "ck." The "k" sound at the end of a word is spelled "ck," if it follows a short vowel.

back	always
black	begin
check	both
rock	favorite
stick	through

Reading Unit 28

Practice reading these sentences.

1. Grandma will come <u>back</u> to visit soon.
2. The color <u>black</u> looks good on you.
3. Did you <u>check</u> to see if your work is neat?
4. I am too small to move that big <u>rock</u>.
5. The dog likes to fetch the <u>stick</u>.

Write each word three times.

back_____

black_____

check_____

rock_____

stick_____

Make up a new sentence for each phonics pattern word.

back_____

black_____

check_____

rock_____

stick_____

Reading Unit 28

Practice reading these sentences.

1. You should <u>always</u> use your manners.
2. It is time for the football game to <u>begin</u>.
3. I'd like <u>both</u> of you to have lunch with us.
4. What is your <u>favorite</u> thing to do?
5. Are you <u>through</u> with your chores?

Write each word three times.

always_____

begin_____

both_____

favorite_____

through_____

Make up a new sentence for each sight word.

always_____

begin_____

both_____

favorite_____

through_____

Practice reading this poem.
Draw a picture to go with it.   Name_____

Kick a Little Rock

Kick a little rock just to
Watch it roll away from you.
Pick up a little stick just to see
How far you can throw it.
These are "kid things" to do that
Grownups just don't understand.

Reading Unit 29

The left column has words which follow a phonics pattern.
The right column has sight words which must be memorized.

Phonics Pattern: Learn the sound of "ing."

being	along
bring	guess
going	next
king	own
thing	page

Reading Unit 29

Name_____

Practice reading these sentences.

1. Thank you for <u>being</u> so helpful.

2. You may <u>bring</u> a friend too.

3. Where are you <u>going</u> after school?

4. I just read a story about a rich <u>king</u>.

5. Move that <u>thing</u> out of the way.

Write each word three times.

being_____

bring_____

going_____

king_____

thing_____

Make up a new sentence for each phonics pattern word.

being_____

bring_____

going_____

king_____

thing_____

Reading Unit 29

Name_____

Practice reading these sentences.

1. I enjoy walking <u>along</u> the coast.
2. Can you <u>guess</u> my age?
3. What school will you go to <u>next</u> year?
4. Someday I hope to <u>own</u> some land.
5. Always read the directions on each <u>page</u>.

Write each word three times.

along_____

guess_____

next_____

own_____

page_____

Make up a new sentence for each sight word.

along_____

guess_____

next_____

own_____

page_____

Practice reading this poem.
Draw a picture to go with it.   Name_____

Spring

Winter is going and it looks like spring.
What kind of weather will it bring?
I think spring is a wonderful thing.
The flowers come out and all the birds sing.

Reading Unit 30

The left column has words which follow a phonics pattern.
The right column has sight words which must be memorized.

Phonics Pattern: Learn the sound of "oi."

coin	birthday
join	hear
noise	special
point	though
voice	wash

Reading Unit 30

<u>Phonics Pattern Words</u>   Name_____

Practice reading these sentences.

1. I found this rare <u>coin</u> on the ground.

2. Would you like to <u>join</u> me for lunch?

3. That dog makes too much <u>noise</u> at night.

4. It is not polite to <u>point</u> at others.

5. Kate has a very good singing <u>voice</u>.

Write each word three times.

coin_____

join_____

noise_____

point_____

voice_____

Make up a new sentence for each phonics pattern word.

coin_____

join_____

noise_____

point_____

voice_____

Reading Unit 30

Name_____

Practice reading these sentences.

1. Where would you like to go on your <u>birthday</u>?
2. Do you <u>hear</u> the birds singing?
3. You have always been a very <u>special</u> friend.
4. I will help clean even <u>though</u> I'm very tired.
5. Now it's time to help <u>wash</u> the dishes.

Write each word three times.

birthday_____

hear_____

special_____

though_____

wash_____

Make up a new sentence for each sight word.

birthday_____

hear_____

special_____

though_____

wash_____

Practice reading this poem.
Draw a picture to go with it.   Name_____

A Voice of Summer

When crickets sing their chirping song,
And frogs can be heard right at dawn,
A voice says summer.
Waves are crashing on the beach,
Good times are never out of reach,
A voice says summer.

Reading Unit 31

The left column has words which follow a phonics pattern.
The right column has sight words which must be memorized.

Phonics Pattern: Learn the sound of "dr."

draw	brother
dress	cousin
drink	father
drop	mother
dry	sister

STEP BY STEP PHONICS

Reading Unit 31

Practice reading these sentences.

1. Do you know how to <u>draw</u> a dog?

2. I like your pretty white <u>dress</u>.

3. What would you like to <u>drink</u>?

4. Be careful not to <u>drop</u> the box.

5. The hot sun made the ground very <u>dry</u>.

Write each word three times.

draw_____

dress_____

drink_____

drop_____

dry_____

Make up a new sentence for each phonics pattern word.

draw_____

dress_____

drink_____

drop_____

dry_____

Reading Unit 31

<u>Sight Words</u>   Name_____

Practice reading these sentences.

1. My little <u>brother</u> will be five next month.
2. I have a <u>cousin</u> who is a famous singer.
3. My <u>father</u> is a manager of a large health club.
4. My <u>mother</u> is an author of many books.
5. My <u>sister</u> is a fifth grade teacher.

Write each word three times.

brother_____

cousin_____

father_____

mother_____

sister_____

Make up a new sentence for each sight word.

brother_____

cousin_____

father_____

mother_____

sister_____

STEP BY STEP PHONICS

Practice reading this poem.
Draw a picture to go with it.   Name_____

Rain Drops

Drip, drop, drip, drop, down comes the rain.
It looks like my plans have been changed once again.
But not for very long, here comes the sun,
To dry up the rain so we'll all have fun!

Reading Unit 32

The left column has words which follow a phonics pattern.
The right column has sight words which must be memorized.

Phonics Pattern: Learn the sound of "tr."

tree	air
tried	animal
trouble	clothes
truck	letter
true	sincerely

Reading Unit 32

Name_____

Practice reading these sentences.

1. The leaves on the <u>tree</u> are turning red and yellow.
2. I am pleased to see you <u>tried</u> your best today.
3. If you follow the rules, you will stay out of <u>trouble</u>.
4. Chad recently bought a new black <u>truck</u>.
5. Is it <u>true</u> that you won a trip to Hawaii?

Write each word three times.

tree_____

tried_____

trouble_____

truck_____

true_____

Make up a new sentence for each phonics pattern word.

tree_____

tried_____

trouble_____

truck_____

true_____

Reading Unit 32

Sight Words

Name_____

Practice reading these sentences.

1. The <u>air</u> up in the mountains is very clean.
2. I saw a strange <u>animal</u> along the road.
3. You sure have a lot of pretty <u>clothes</u>.
4. It is fun to get a <u>letter</u> from a friend.
5. A business letter often ends with <u>sincerely</u>.

Write each word three times.

air_____

animal_____

clothes_____

letter_____

sincerely_____

Make up a new sentence for each sight word.

air_____

animal_____

clothes_____

letter_____

sincerely_____

Practice reading this poem.
Draw a picture to go with it.   Name_____

Oh Beautiful Tree

A Christmas tree is a beautiful sight,
Giving hope and cheer to a winter night.
Now what's in that package?
I tried to see,
Maybe a train, truck, or trike for me.

Reading Unit 33

The left column has words which follow a phonics pattern.
The right column has sight words which must be memorized.

Phonics Pattern: Learn the sound of "ew."

few	asked
grew	eye
knew	high
new	learn
threw	still

STEP BY STEP PHONICS

Reading Unit 33

Name_____

Practice reading these sentences.

1. A <u>few</u> relatives will be here for the holidays.
2. My sister <u>grew</u> a lot since last year.
3. I <u>knew</u> you'd have fun at the party.
4. Is that a <u>new</u> coat you have on?
5. The baseball player <u>threw</u> the ball fast.

Write each word three times.

few_____

grew_____

knew_____

new_____

threw_____

Make up a new sentence for each phonics pattern word.

few_____

grew_____

knew_____

new_____

threw_____

Reading Unit 33

Name_____

Practice reading these sentences.

1. Dad <u>asked</u> me to help you clean the garage.
2. It feels like I have something in my <u>eye.</u>
3. That jar is too <u>high</u> for me to reach.
4. It is important to stay in school and <u>learn</u>.
5. You need to sit <u>still</u> while I take your picture.

Write each word three times.

asked_____

eye_____

high_____

learn_____

still_____

Make up a new sentence for each sight word.

asked_____

eye_____

high_____

learn_____

still_____

Practice reading this poem.
Draw a picture to go with it.   Name_____

Who Knew?

Jack had a bean seed and didn't know what to do.
He didn't really want it, so out the window it flew.
That magic bean seed just grew and grew.
When it would stop nobody knew.

Reading Unit 34

The left column has words which follow a phonics pattern.
The right column has sight words which must be memorized.

Phonics Pattern: Learn the sound of "aw."

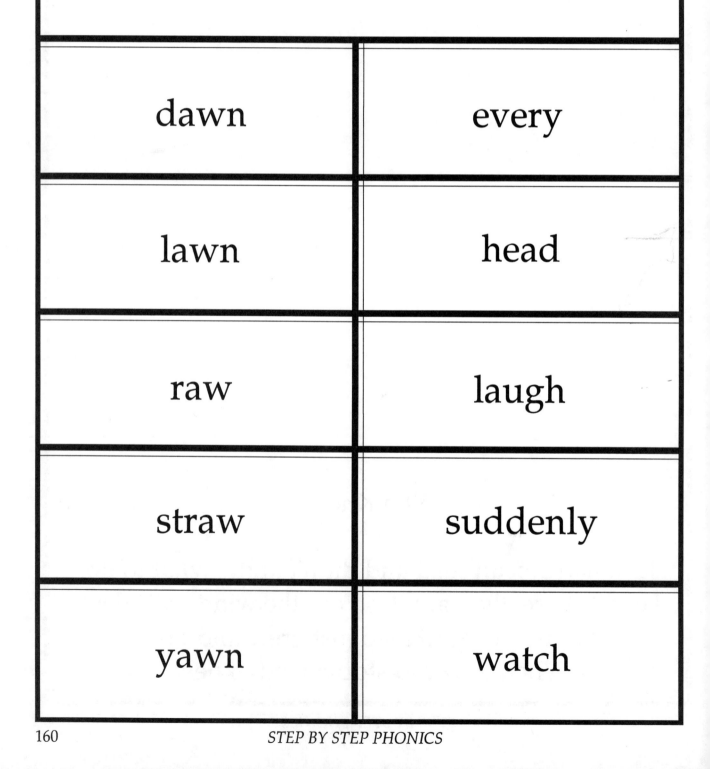

dawn	every
lawn	head
raw	laugh
straw	suddenly
yawn	watch

STEP BY STEP PHONICS

Reading Unit 34

Phonics Pattern Words   Name_____

Practice reading these sentences.

1. We'll get up at <u>dawn</u> to go camping.
2. Brian will mow the <u>lawn</u> on Saturday.
3. Eating <u>raw</u> vegetables is a healthy snack.
4. Will you bring me another <u>straw</u> for my milk?
5. It is rude to <u>yawn</u> when someone is speaking.

Write each word three times.

dawn_____

lawn_____

raw_____

straw_____

yawn_____

Make up a new sentence for each phonics pattern word.

dawn_____

lawn_____

raw_____

straw_____

yawn_____

Reading Unit 34

Name_____

Practice reading these sentences.

1. Every student in this class is smart.
2. That hat is too small for my head.
3. The clown made the kids laugh.
4. It suddenly started raining during our picnic.
5. I need a new battery for my watch.

Write each word three times.

every_____

head_____

laugh_____

suddenly_____

watch_____

Make up a new sentence for each sight word.

every_____

head_____

laugh_____

suddenly_____

watch_____

Practice reading this poem.
Draw a picture to go with it.   Name_____

Stop That Yawn

Please don't yawn when someone is talking to you.
It doesn't matter if you are bored to tears.
It doesn't matter is it's dawn, midnight, or
If you haven't slept for two years.
It's just not polite.

Reading Unit 35

The left column has words which follow a phonics pattern.
The right column has sight words which must be memorized.

Phonics Pattern: Learn the sound of "au."

author	answer
caught	children
daughter	often
pause	together
taught	until

Reading Unit 35

<u>Phonics Pattern Words</u>   Name_____

Practice reading these sentences.

1. You might be an <u>author</u> when you grow up.
2. I think I <u>caught</u> this cold over the weekend.
3. My wonderful <u>daughter</u> is named Victoria.
4. Sometimes it's important to <u>pause</u> and just relax.
5. This program <u>taught</u> me how to read and spell.

Write each word three times.

author_____

caught_____

daughter_____

pause_____

taught_____

Make up a new sentence for each phonics pattern word.

author_____

caught_____

daughter_____

pause_____

taught_____

Reading Unit 35

Name_____

Practice reading these sentences.

1. Do you know the <u>answer</u> to this question?
2. The <u>children</u> had fun at the party.
3. Do you go to the park very <u>often</u>?
4. If we work <u>together</u>, we'll have a great year.
5. Never wait <u>until</u> the last minute to study.

Write each word three times.

answer_____

children_____

often_____

together_____

until_____

Make up a new sentence for each sight word.

answer_____

children_____

often_____

together_____

until_____

Practice reading this poem.
Draw a picture to go with it.   Name_____

Almost Caught

The first fish that I caught was bigger than a horse.
I tried to reel it in. It got away, of course.
This author sat and waited,
For the next to bite the hook.
But after many hours gave it up to read a book.

Reading Unit 36

The left column has words which follow a phonics pattern.
The right column has sight words which must be memorized.

Phonics Pattern: Learn the sound of "ur."

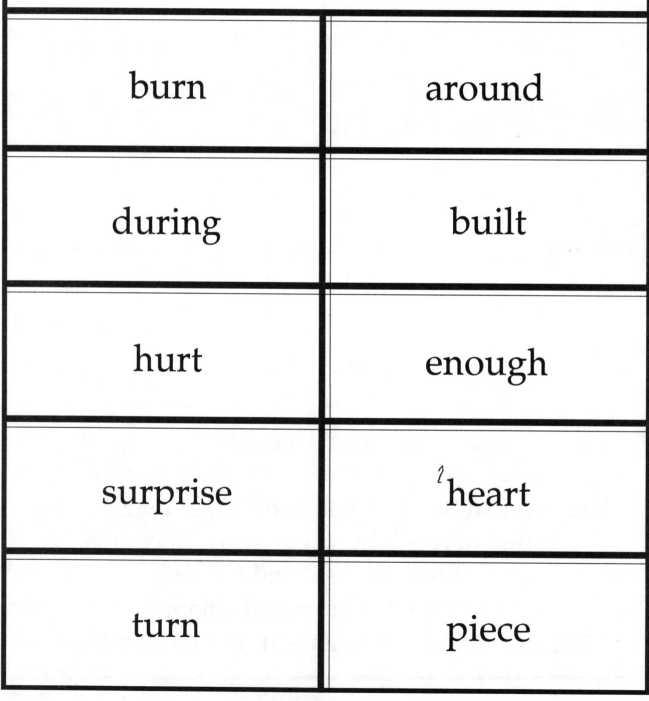

burn	around
during	built
hurt	enough
surprise	[2] heart
turn	piece

STEP BY STEP PHONICS

Reading Unit 36

Practice reading these sentences.

1. Be careful not to <u>burn</u> yourself.
2. Nicole fell asleep <u>during</u> the show.
3. I <u>hurt</u> my arm playing tennis.
4. There is a <u>surprise</u> for you in the kitchen.
5. Make sure you <u>turn</u> off the light.

Write each word three times.

burn_____

during_____

hurt_____

surprise_____

turn_____

Make up a new sentence for each phonics pattern word.

burn_____

during_____

hurt_____

surprise_____

turn_____

Reading Unit 36

Name_____

Practice reading these sentences.

1. Mike and I jogged <u>around</u> the track.
2. Last summer dad <u>built</u> a tree house for us.
3. Did you have <u>enough</u> time to finish?
4. Let me show you how to make a <u>heart</u>.
5. This puzzle is missing one <u>piece</u>.

Write each word three times.

around_____

built_____

enough_____

heart_____

piece_____

Make up a new sentence for each sight word.

around_____

built_____

enough_____

heart_____

piece_____

Practice reading this poem.
Draw a picture to go with it.   Name_____

What's the Surprise?

If someone told you on a certain day,
There is no longer a month called May.
The green, green grass has all turned yellow,
And streets everywhere turned into jello,
Surprise, it must be April Fool's Day!

Reading Unit 37

The left column has words which follow a phonics pattern.
The right column has sight words which must be memorized.

Phonics Pattern: Learn the sound of "tion."

dictionary	again
education	already
information	country
question	heard
vacation	second

Reading Unit 37

Practice reading these sentences.

1. If you don't know how to spell a word, use a <u>dictionary</u>.
2. Getting a good <u>education</u> helps you become successful.
3. I need some <u>information</u> for the local newspaper.
4. Does anyone have a <u>question</u> about the test tomorrow?
5. I hope you have a fun summer <u>vacation</u>.

Write each word three times.

dictionary_____

education_____

information_____

question_____

vacation_____

Make up a new sentence for each phonics pattern word.

dictionary_____

education_____

information_____

question_____

vacation_____

Reading Unit 37

Name_____

Practice reading these sentences.

1. Will you please open the door for me <u>again</u>?

2. I have <u>already</u> seen that movie.

3. We have a lot of opportunity in our <u>country</u>.

4. Have you <u>heard</u> the wonderful news?

5. I really enjoyed being in <u>second</u> grade.

Write each word three times.

again_____

already_____

country_____

heard_____

second_____

Make up a new sentence for each sight word.

again_____

already_____

country_____

heard_____

second_____

Practice reading this poem.
Draw a picture to go with it.   Name_____

Use the Dictionary

If spelling just isn't your cup of tea,
This is what you must do, now listen to me!
Whether at home, in school, or on vacation,
A dictionary give you the information.

Reading Unit 38

The left column has words which follow a phonics pattern.
The right column has sight words which must be memorized.

Phonics Pattern: Learn the sound of "ture."

adventure	above
furniture	mountain
future	possible
nature	world
picture	young

Reading Unit 38

Practice reading these sentences.

1. You can go on an <u>adventure</u> by reading a book.
2. Will you help me carry in the new <u>furniture</u>?
3. You will have a great <u>future</u>, if you stay in school.
4. There is a lot of beauty in <u>nature</u>.
5. What happened to the <u>picture</u> that was here?

Write each word three times.

adventure_____

furniture_____

future_____

nature_____

picture_____

Make up a new sentence for each phonics pattern word.

adventure_____

furniture_____

future_____

nature_____

picture_____

Reading Unit 38

Practice reading these sentences.

1. Look at that pretty picture <u>above</u> the fireplace.
2. We climbed all the way to the top of the <u>mountain</u>.
3. Will it be <u>possible</u> for you to come early?
4. There are many kind people in this <u>world</u>.
5. When I was <u>young</u>, I liked to fly kites.

Write each word three times.

above_____

mountain_____

possible_____

world_____

young_____

Make up a new sentence for each sight word.

above_____

mountain_____

possible_____

world_____

young_____

Practice reading this poem.
Draw a picture to go with it.   Name_____

My Adventure

My adventure first began,
When I learned to read and write.
Once you learn to read,
You can learn everything in sight!
Plan for your life as you want it to be.
Work for your goals and live joyfully.

Reading Unit 39

The left column has words which follow a phonics pattern.
The right column has sight words which must be memorized.

Phonics Pattern: Learn the sound of "sion."

confusion	cough
decision	earth
occasion	music
permission	never
television	under

STEP BY STEP PHONICS

Reading Unit 39

<u>Phonics Pattern Words</u>   Name_____

Practice reading these sentences.

1. The earthquake caused a lot of <u>confusion</u>.
2. I finally made a <u>decision</u> about what to buy.
3. Having a baby is a very special <u>occasion</u>.
4. Do I have your <u>permission</u> to leave school early?
5. Always do your homework before watching <u>television</u>.

Write each word three times.

confusion_____

decision_____

occasion_____

permission_____

television_____

Make up a new sentence for each phonics pattern word.

confusion_____

decision_____

occasion_____

permission_____

television_____

Reading Unit 39

<u>Sight Words</u>   Name_____

Practice reading these sentences.

1. It sounds like you have a bad <u>cough</u>.
2. We need to take good care of our <u>earth</u>.
3. What kind of <u>music</u> do you listen to?
4. I have <u>never</u> tried ice skating.
5. The long tunnel took us <u>under</u> the mountain.

Write each word three times.

cough_____

earth_____

music_____

never_____

under_____

Make up a new sentence for each sight word.

cough_____

earth_____

music_____

never_____

under_____

Practice reading this poem.
Draw a picture to go with it.   Name_____

Instead of Television

Instead of television, make the decision to
Read an exciting adventure story.
Get permission to play in the park.
Make some time to visit a lonely person.
See the beautiful things nature has to offer.
There is a real world just waiting to be discovered
And it's not behind a glass screen!

Reading Unit 40

The left column has words which follow a phonics pattern.
The right column has sight words which must be memorized.

Phonics Pattern: The letter "c" makes the "s" sound when it is followed by "e" or "i."

celebration	excellent
center	happened
certain	honest
circle	hour
city	problem

Reading Unit 40

Practice reading these sentences.

1. A wedding is a wonderful <u>celebration</u>.
2. That is a beautiful vase on the <u>center</u> of your table.
3. Are you <u>certain</u> your father will let you go?
4. All of you need to form a <u>circle</u> for the game.
5. I think San Francisco is a beautiful <u>city</u>.

Write each word three times.

celebration_____

center_____

certain_____

circle_____

city_____

Make up a new sentence for each phonics pattern word.

celebration_____

center_____

certain_____

circle_____

city_____

Reading Unit 40

Name_____

Practice reading these sentences.

1. You did an <u>excellent</u> job learning this entire program!
2. I wondered what <u>happened</u> when you were late.
3. It is good to be an <u>honest</u> person.
4. The train will be leaving in one <u>hour</u>.
5. By now, you certainly don't have a reading <u>problem</u>!

Write each word three times.

excellent_____

happened_____

honest_____

hour_____

problem_____

Make up a new sentence for each sight word.

excellent_____

happened_____

honest_____

hour_____

problem_____

Practice reading this poem.
Draw a picture to go with it.   Name_____

The City

The city is covered with fog today,
All around and over the bay.
A certain excitement fills the air,
Of factories, theaters, and movie stars there.

Congratulations, you made it through
Step by Step Phonics!

Now you know the secret to success for reading or anything you do in life! What is it, you ask? Stop and think about it for a moment. Was it easy going through all of the reading units, doing the writing activities, and learning to read and spell all the words? Of course not, but it was certainly worth it! The secret???

Success in life requires one major thing:

Hard Work

"The road to success is paved with hard work, believing in yourself, and determination to reach your goals."

Laurie Lee Bell, 1998
(Author, Teacher, Wife, Parent, Runner, Friend)

The "Be a Winner" chart is only effective if it is really a part of your belief system. Positive, goal oriented teachers pass on enthusiasm and a desire for learning to their students. When students have the "I can" attitude, their learning soars. If desired, you may modify the "Be a Winner" chart to your belief system.

Organization

Students are more effective learners when they're organized. You must teach your students organizational skills. I physically demonstrated how to organize a student's messy desk. My rule was, "No loose papers in your desk." If students wanted the papers, they had to take them home each day. If not, I taught them to throw them away. Set aside a few minutes daily for students to clean their desks and straighten up the room. Teaching students to be organized is a highly valuable life skill.

It is a good idea to take some time and assess your own organization. If you file things immediately, it will ultimately save you a lot of time. Use the time you give students each day, for straightening up, to get your own things in order. It is much easier to present lessons effectively when you know precisely where everything is.

Responsibility

Teaching children responsibility definitely helps create a highly effective classroom. The primary way I instilled responsibility was by giving each student a job to do each month. Think of yourself as a manager with 30 employees. By delegating the smaller jobs, you will be a more productive teacher, with more time to concentrate on the important job of teaching lessons. The students benefit by becoming responsible as they learn to take care of their desks and classroom.

Each of my 30 first grade students had a job. Students had to write job application letters on the first day of each month. Students with the best letters received the job of their choice. When students had equally good letters but wanted the same job, I'd actually interview them briefly. This taught them real life skills plus helped me pick the best student for a particular job. Occasionally I'd pick a student for a job whose letter wasn't the best to encourage a beginning, struggling writer.

When you start the school year, it is important that you explain the expectations for each job. For example, desk inspectors look for messy desks in their row that need to be organized. As the classroom manager, it is up to you to enforce that each student does his or her job. Once students get used to having jobs they get quite proficient at doing them.

These are some jobs my students have done over the years: line leader, flag leader, pencil sharpener emptier, sink cleaner, board cleaner, office monitor, classroom door person, listeners, library door person, marble jar person, light monitor, sweepers, desk monitors, paper passers, helpers, name checkers, and game monitor. To create enough jobs for everyone, you can have as many helpers, listeners, sweepers, or desk inspectors as necessary.

My students really looked forward to writing job letters each month and getting a new job. You can create a very special bulletin board featuring the jobs. Take each student's picture and place it over the job's title. Gve the students an award certificate when they are chosen for the classroom job they wanted.

Discuss the concepts of responsibility and teamwork with your students. If someone is absent, ask for volunteers to take over that student's job for the day. When everyone is doing their job efficiently, point out how smoothly the class operates. Occasionally, surprise the class with a few bonus minutes stating it's because they saved so much time through their teamwork. This will encourage the camaraderie to continue.

Show a Sincere Interest in Each Child

This is one of the most important principles in creating a highly effective classroom. Be sincerely interested in each one of your students. Show them the concern you would give to your own child. Be interested in their accomplishments.

Some students are a little more challenging to show a sincere interest in. However, when you as the adult reach out and treat them kindly first, in time they will respond to you in a positive manner. Students want to know their teacher likes them. Students want to feel, "My teacher really does care how I do." Just knowing that the teacher cares can change the course of a student's entire life.

Discipline with respect. Organization. A winning attitude. Responsibility. A sincere interest. These principles will be invaluable in your teaching.

8

Choosing Quality Literature

It is very important to share quality literature with beginning readers in order for them to realize just how fun reading can be! Literature may also be used to teach concepts in science, math, and social studies. By using stories that teach concepts, students are gaining reading practice and learning important information at the same time! The picture books in this chapter are labeled by reading levels and categories.

Reading Level 1=RL1
Reading Level 2=RL2
Reading Level 3=RL3

(C)-Concept

There are many books which teach concepts including colors, numbers, opposites, shapes, parts of speech, and letter sounds. Other concept books may be used to enhance your teaching in core curriculum areas such as social studies and science.

(P)-Predictable/Pattern

The repetition of the words makes reading easier.

(W)-Wordless

(JPF)-Just Plain Fun

These books may be the key to creating lifelong readers. Once students realize reading is enjoyable, they are more motivated to want to read. Motivated readers learn to read much faster!

If you are working with students who are only reading at Level 1, you may still read a more difficult story with them and have them do a follow up writing activity. Often, more difficult stories are more interesting. Therefore, it would be a good idea to share some "JPF" stories right away to really motivate them to want to learn how to read by themselves!

The following books are available at bookstores, school supply stores, or through educational catalogs. Also, libraries have an excellent selection plus librarians are generally very helpful and will direct you to the area where particular books may be found.

An excellent strategy for making books "come alive" is to have students do writing activities which relate to the story.

RL1 (P) Martin, B. (1983). *Brown Bear, Brown Bear, What Do You See?*

This story is easy to read because it has a predictable pattern. After students are familiar with the pattern, they may create a similar story using the same or different characters. You may have them change the characters in the story to the names of people they know. Students really enjoy this activity.

RL1 (C) Dr. Seuss. (1963). *Dr. Seuss's ABC*

Use this book to teach students the sounds of the alphabet letters. Point out that the vowel sounds for a, e, i, o, and u, represent the short vowel sound, which is why I chose this book. After they are familiar with each letter's sound, you may have them create an "ABC" book with their own picture idea for each letter. You may have them write a sentence such as: A is for apple. This would also be a good time to include handwriting practice for each letter.

RL1 (C) Garne, S.T. (1992). *One White Sail*

This is an excellent story for teaching the concept of numbers to ten. After reading it students can make their own numbers to ten book. Examples: three girls dancing, five red windows...

RL1 (C) Hutchins, P. (1968). *Rosie's Walk*

Have the students write a similar story and have them include prepositions such as over, under, and through.

RL1 (C, P) LeSieg, T. (1961). *Ten Apples Up On Top*

Have the students draw a picture with up to ten apples on top of themselves and label with their name. An example for this story: Brian has nine apples up on top.

RL1 (JPF, W) Wiesner, D. (1991). *Tuesday*

Wordless books are an excellent way to allow children to tell in their own words, exactly what is happening on each page. For beginning readers and writers, you may write their ideas on sticky notes and adhere to each page. For students who have gone through several reading units, they will be able to write their own thoughts.

RL2 (P) Hutchins, P. (1986). *The Doorbell Rang*

After the students are familiar with the story, have them write a new ending. An example for this story: The doorbell rang but it was not grandma. It was...

RL2 (C) Bannatyne Cugnet, J. (1992). *A Prairie Alphabet*

This book has beautiful, realistic pictures of life on the prairie. It could be incorporated into a unit on farming or life in the Midwest. Students could make their own ABC books featuring prairie life. Example: H is for horses eating hay.

RL2 (C, P) Carle, E. (1987). *The Very Hungry Caterpillar*

Have students list and illustrate the various stages in the life cycle of a butterfly.

RL3 (C, JPF) Viorst, J. (1972). *Alexander and the Terrible, Horrible, No Good, Very Bad Day*

Discuss the importance of never giving up on a "bad day" by always looking for good in each situation. Help students to understand how having a positive attitude is beneficial to them and everyone around them. List the reasons a positive attitude is beneficial. Examples: more friends, feeling happier...

RL3 (JPF) Barrett, J. (1978). *Cloudy With a Chance of Meatballs*

Students really love this story and you might too! Have them draw a rain scene with all types of food coming out of the sky. Real types of dry food could be glued on including macaroni, rice, or oatmeal. Then students should describe their picture. An example: It rained pancakes with butter and syrup followed by pitchers of orange juice. Eggs landed on cars and people. A severe rice storm blew across the valley!

RL3 (C) Marzollo, J. (1993). *Happy Birthday, Martin Luther King*

Discuss Martin Luther King's life and the contributions of this American hero. Discuss the many sacrifices he went through to achieve equality for all people. The students could make a booklet depicting different aspects of his life and describe each scene. Next, have the students write a dream for their future with the steps it will take to make their dream come true. Point out that dreams must be accompanied by action.

RL3 (C, JPF) Hall ETS, M. (1978). *Gilberto and the Wind*
Use this book as part of a science lesson on wind. Discuss the effects of strong winds such as tornadoes and hurricanes. Brainstorm ways wind is useful. Examples: drying clothes, windmill power...Make individual or a class book of wind facts.

RL3 (C) Say, A. (1993). *Grandfather's Journey*
This book could be used to introduce a social studies unit on the many cultures in America. Discuss the feelings of honor, loyalty, and respect the grandfather had for both Japan and America.

RL3 (C, JPF) Hoberman, M. (1978). *A House Is a House for Me*
Discuss all of the different types of houses for things in the story. Then have the students think of different things and what a house would be for them. An example: An ocean is a home for a shark.

RL3 (C) Brandenberg, A. (1992). *I'm Growing*
Have students draw themselves at different stages in their lives and label. Example: This is when I was a baby.

RL3 (JPF) Babcock, C. (1993). *No Moon, No Milk*
Students will enjoy this ridiculous story about a very determined cow. After reading the story, teach students the correct way to write a letter. Have them write letters to "Mrs. Cow" asking her various questions. Perhaps you can respond to their letters!

RL3 (JPF) Van Allsburg, C. (1985). *The Polar Express*
Students of all ages will love to hear this true classic around Christmas time. After enjoying the story, have students do a holiday art project depicting a scene from the story.

RL3 (C, JPF) Keats, E. J. (1962). *The Snowy Day*
After reading this story, have students make paper snowflakes. Then, teach them how to write a Japanese haiku poem, a three line

poem about nature. The first and third lines have 5 syllables, the second line has 7 syllables. Attach the snowflakes and poems to construction paper and display. Example: Snow is falling down.

> Looks like winter once again.
> Time to bundle up!

RL3 (JPF) Scieszka, J. (1989). *The True Story of the 3 Little Pigs!*

Students really love this story and you will too! An excellent way to teach students to write stories is by doing a unit on fairy tales. After reading several versions of each fairy tale, have students write their own.

RL3 (JPF) Sendak, M. (1963). *Where the Wild Things Are*

This would be a good story for a "Monster" poem. Discuss all the different types of monsters: red, green, black, spotted, scary, mean, nice, and so on. Then demonstrate how to write a poem using the different adjectives. An example: **Monsters**

> Mean monsters,
> Nice monsters,
> Red and green monsters,
> Big and small monsters,
> Nice monsters too.

An important goal is to get students to become lifelong readers. Sharing some of these books will help accomplish that goal. There are so many excellent books available which lead to great writing activities, teach concepts, or are just plain fun to read. Following are additional titles to guide you when making future selections.

Reading Level 1
(C) Martin, B. (1989). *Chicka Chicka Boom Boom*
(C, JPF) Clements, A. (1997). *Double Trouble in Walla Walla*
(P) Christelow, E. (1989). *Five Little Monkeys Jumping on the Bed*
(C) Carle, E. (1998). *Hello, Red Fox*
(JPF) Dr. Seuss. (1991). *Hop On Pop*
(JPF) Winter, S. (1993). *Me Too*
(C, JPF) Hutchins, P. (1993). *My Best Friend*
(W) de Paola, T. (1990). *Pancakes For Breakfast*
(P) Martin, B. (1991). *Polar Bear, Polar Bear, What Do You Hear?*

(C, JPF) Richardson, J. (1992). *Ten Bears in a Bed*
(P, JPF) Miranda, A. (1997). *To Market, To Market*
(P) Harter, D. (1997). *Walking Through the Jungle*

Reading Level 2
(C) Jordan, S. (1996). *Down on Casey's Farm*
(C) Silverstein, S. (1964). *The Giving Tree*
(JPF) Dr. Seuss. (1960). *Green Eggs and Ham*
(P, JPF) Joffe Numeroff, L. (1991). *If You Give a Moose a Muffin*
(C) Lionni, L. (1960). *Inch by Inch*
(JPF) Degen, B. (1983). *Jamberry*
(C) Mayer, M. (1994). *Just Lost!*
(P) Wood, A. (1984). *The Napping House*
(JPF) Freeman, D. (1987). *A Rainbow of My Own*
(JPF) Mayer, M. (1988). *There's Something in My Attic*
(P, JPF) Taback, S. (1997). *There Was an Old Lady Who Swallowed a Fly*

Reading Level 3
(JPF) Lionni, L. (1969). *Alexander and the Wind-Up Mouse*
(JPF) Parish, P. (1994). *Amelia Bedelia and the Surprise Shower*
(C) Hoffman, M. (1995). *Boundless Grace*
(JPF) Freeman, D. (1986). *Corduroy*
(C) Hall Ets, M. (1978). *Gilberto and the Wind*
(C, P) Carle, E. (1977). *The Grouchy Ladybug*
(C, P) Munsch, R. (1989). *Love You, Forever*
(C) de Paola, T. (1988). *Legend of the Indian Paintbrush*
(JPF) McCloskey, R. (1969). *Make Way For Ducklings*
(C) Frasier, D. (1991). *On the Day You Were Born*
(JPF) Steig, W. (1969). *Sylvester and the Magic Pebble*
(JPF) Potter, B. (1987). *The Tale of Peter Rabbit*
(C) Johnson, A. (1990). *When I Am Old With You*

Helpful Spelling Strategies

Explain to the students that a suffix is an ending added to a word. Learning a few, simple strategies for adding suffixes will greatly increase the students' spelling and writing ability. After each strategy, have the students add the suffixes to the practice words. These spelling strategies should be reviewed once a week. You may want to give additional practice words.

Strategy One: When adding suffixes to words that end with a consonant and y, change the y to i, then add the suffix.

Examples: happy>happier happy>happiest happy>happiness
beauty>beautiful lucky>luckily fly>flies try>tries
Practice words: Add **er** and **est** to happy, funny, and silly.
Add **ed** to cry and dry.

Strategy Two: When adding suffixes to words ending with a vowel-consonant-silent e: Drop the e, then add the suffix.

Examples: like>liked bike>biking bake>baked bake>baking
bake>baker refuse>refused refuse>refusing
Practice words: Add **er** and **ing** to dive, hike and drive.
Add **er** and **est** to nice. Add **ing** to hope.

Strategy Three: When adding suffixes to words ending with a consonant-vowel-consonant: Double the final consonant, then add the suffix.

Examples: hop>hopped hop>hopping run>running run>runner
stop>stopped stop>stopping

Practice words: Add **ed** and **ing** to drop, mop, and shop.
Add **er** and **est** to hot. Add **ing** to sit.

Strategy Four: Making Words Plural
A) If a word ends with a vowel and y, just add s.

Examples: day>days key>keys toy>toys
Practice words: play, stay, donkey, boy

B) If a word ends in ch, sh, ss, or x, add es.

Examples: witch>witches dish>dishes glass>glasses
Practice words: church, wish, miss, box

C) If a word ends in f or fe, change the f or fe to v, add es.

Examples: half>halves knife>knives life>lives
Practice words: wolf, elf, wife, calf

Whenever the students are writing, encourage them to use these spelling strategies. Other skills which should be taught include: proofreading, using quotation marks, ABC order, punctuation, contractions, compound words, handwriting, homonyms, prefixes, suffixes, and detailed writing both fiction and nonfiction.

Answers
Strategy One: happier, happiest, funnier, funniest, sillier, silliest
                cried, dried
Strategy Two: diver, diving, hiker, hiking, driver, driving
                nicer, nicest, hoping
Strategy Three: dropped, dropping, mopped, mopping, shopped,
                shopping, hotter, hottest, sitting
Strategy Four A: plays, stays, donkeys, boys
Strategy Four B: churches, wishes, misses, boxes
Strategy Four C: wolves, elves, wives, calves

Glossary

ABC book: alphabet book, each letter has a picture to represent its sound.

Autobiography: the story of one's life written by that person.

Context: the verbal or written environment in which a word or group of words occur which affect the word's meaning.

Comprehension: an understanding of a book or conversation.

Consonant: a speech sound produced by a partial obstruction of the air stream; all the letters in the alphabet except a, e, i, o, and u.

Dictating: recording one's ideas while another is speaking.

Digraph: a pair of letters representing a single speech sound.

Homonym: one of two or more words that sound the same but have different meanings. *For* and *four* are homonyms.

Paragraph: a group of sentences which tell about one main idea, usually begins with a topic sentence.

Pattern: a repeating group of letters.

Phonics: a method of teaching beginners to read and pronounce words by learning the sounds of letters and letter groups.

Picture book: beginning readers; the pictures usually correspond to the written word.

Plural: more than one of something.

Prediction: to decide ahead of time what will probably happen.

Proofread: to find errors in an original manuscript, mark them, for the purpose of writing over, or publishing.

Reading strategy: any method employed to gain meaning from the written word, including phonics and using context clues.

Sight words: words which must be recognized on sight as most can not be phonetically sounded out. *Eye* and *taught* are sight words.

Suffix: an ending added to a word.

Syllable: a single, uninterrupted sound forming part of a word or the entire word. "Go" has one syllable. "Going" has two syllables.

Vowel: a speech sound produced by the free passage of breath; the letters a, e, i, o, and u.

Whole language: an educational theory that children will learn how to read and spell simply by immersion in the activity, with incidental phonics, spelling, and skills instruction.

CERTIFICATE OF

READING ACHIEVEMENT

AWARDED TO

_____

IN RECOGNITION OF LEARNING TO READ _____ STEP BY STEP PHONICS POEMS

PRESENTED BY _____

ON THIS DATE _____

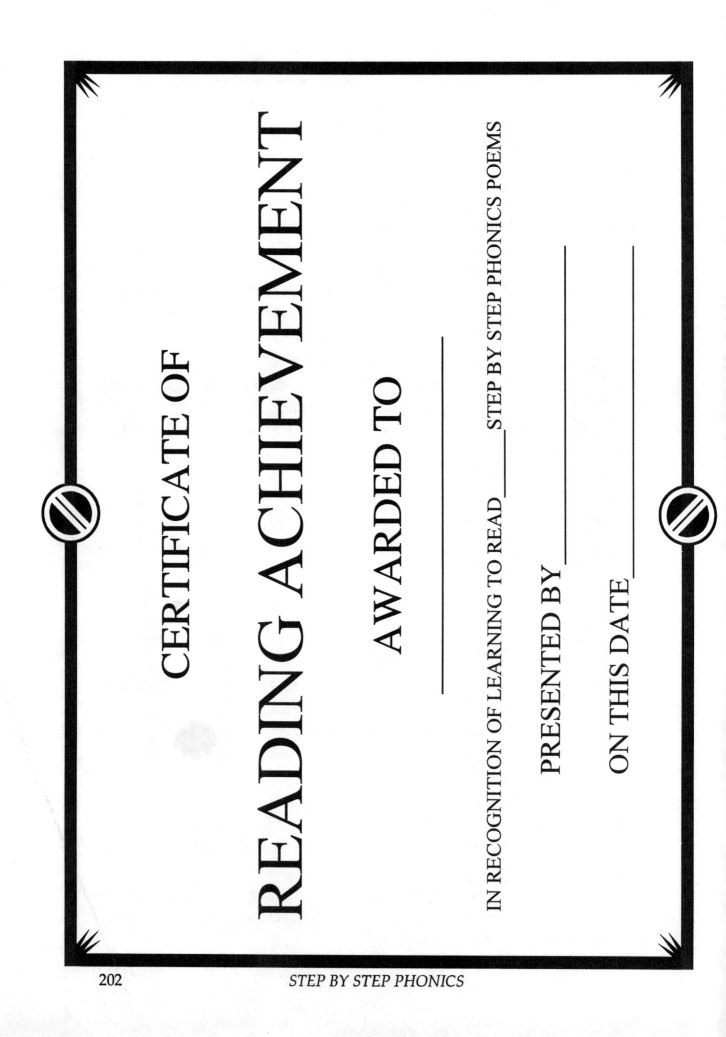

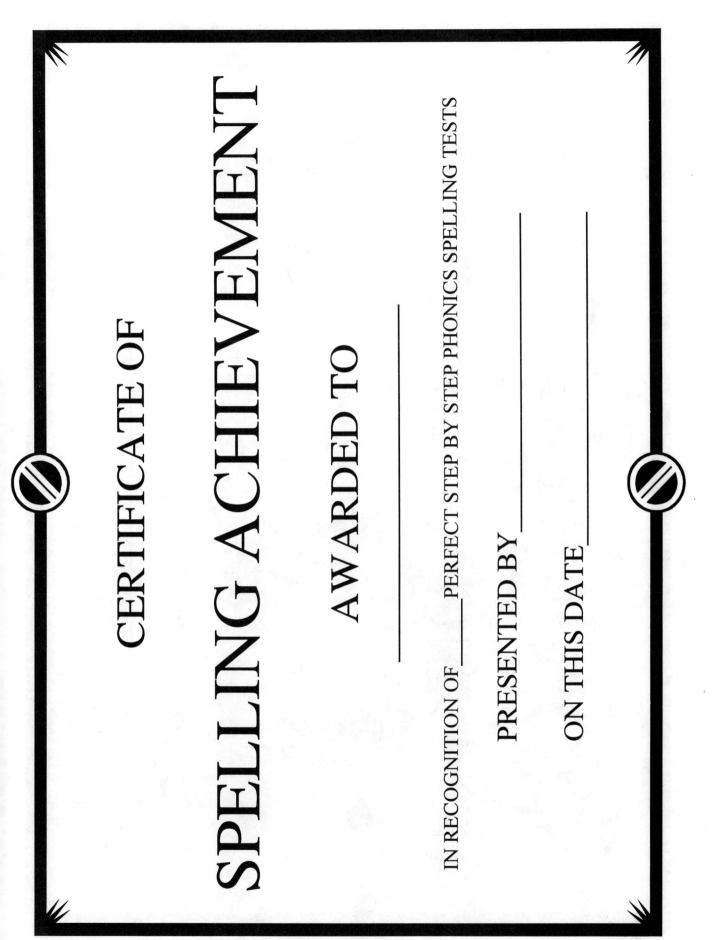

CERTIFICATE OF

SPELLING ACHIEVEMENT

AWARDED TO

_____

IN RECOGNITION OF _____ PERFECT STEP BY STEP PHONICS SPELLING TESTS

PRESENTED BY _____

ON THIS DATE _____

BE A WINNER!

1. I am important.
2. I am in school to learn and get smart.
3. I always do my best.
4. I care about others.
5. I will help others.
6. I am a good listener.
7. I will use my manners.
8. I will work hard.
9. A winner never quits.
10. I will graduate.

EDUCATOR AND PARENT REVIEWS

"...Laurie Lee Bell's an experienced first grade teacher who has combined the best of both 'whole language' and 'phonics' frameworks into a compendium of systematic weekly plans that are highly recommended for both the traditional classroom teacher and the homeschooling parent."
James A. Cox, Editor, Midwest Book Review

"*Step by Step Phonics* is easy to incorporate into my lesson plans. I don't have to hunt for extra materials--everything is right at hand. The program works and the children enjoy it."
Vickie L. Boutiette, 1998 North Dakota Teacher of the Year
Moorhead State University: BS & Valley City State University: MA in Reading

"*Step by Step Phonics* is a wonderful, easy to use program that can be used as a supplement or by itself. It is great to incorporate as a straight forward homework plan. I heard about this program from a friend who teaches special education and he loved it. Thanks for providing a simple and useful product."
Margie Feinberg, Special Education Teacher
South Dakota State University: MA in Special Education, LH & MS Credential

"*Step by Step Phonics* is well organized and a must for the child who needs phonemic strategies or simply a review of phonics concepts on a daily basis. It is easy for a teacher to see success after only a few lessons. As an upper grade teacher, I've found the program easy to implement in small group sessions, as a center activity, or on a one-to-one basis. *Step by Step Phonics* is...an asset to any classroom curriculum."
Lea Joy Shortlidge, Sixth Grade Teacher
University of California, Bakersfield: AA, BA, MA, Reading Specialist Credential

"The program is great! I've been using my own made up list for years, but this is exactly what I would have liked to have written. The use of word families and sight words is indispensable for children---plus the poems! I use them to make quick reading and comprehension checks weekly."
Nicholas Bartolic, Second Grade Teacher
University of California, Irvine: MA in Education, LH & MS Credential

"Laurie Lee Bell...has joined the best of both frameworks...and organized an integrated reading, writing, phonics, and spelling system that will free children to become self-sufficient readers and writers. I recommend this outstanding resource to other educators."
Ruth Martin, Reading and Writing Consultant & Education Course Extension Instructor, University of California, Riverside
California State University, San Bernardino: MA in Education

"The only thing that I changed in my teaching methods from last year to this year was the addition of the *Step by Step Phonics* program. My first graders this year are already reading and writing as much as my first graders were doing at the end of the year last year. This program goes back to the basics, back to what worked in the past."
Robert Schumacher, First Grade Teacher
California State University, San Bernardino

"I am very impressed with how well my son, Frederick has learned to read and write with the *Step by Step Phonics* program. He reads everything and so fast. He sounds out the word if he doesn't already know it. I feel this program is a blessing." **Roslyn Gladney, Parent**

"We are very pleased with the *Step by Step Phonics* program. Samantha has done so well and is very enthusiastic about reading. The program is organized. One week for each unit, so the children can't help but learn." ***Carole Harry, Parent***

"I enjoy the success my students achieve with the use of the program. I have used the program through the year and have only received compliments from parents and students. They enjoy the program. Students can't wait until Friday to take a spelling test!"
Teresa D. Behnke, First Grade Teacher
National University: Masters in Curriculum and Instructional Leadership

"My daughter, Amanda has been using *Step by Step Phonics* since she entered first grade. By the end of the first period, she was already reading. I can't say enough good things about this program. It is fun and easy to understand. I recommend this program to anyone interested in teaching their child to read." ***Debra Benvenuto, Parent***

"My family is very thankful and grateful to the *Step by Step Phonics* program for the great progress that Bianca has had. In six weeks she has learned how to read. Anyone who wants to learn to read in a short time, I strongly suggest "*Step by Step Phonics*."
Gniselda Duran, Parent

"*Step by Step Phonics* is just what the name says. It is a step by step guide to teaching the most important foundation of all our learning--reading. I found the program extremely beneficial."
Renee Daetwiler, First Grade Teacher
Temple University, Philadelphia

"The *Step by Step Phonics* program really is an asset to my twins. It made reading easier and the twins are using their sounds and what they learned from Mrs. Bell's program. Mrs. Bell is also an excellent educator who not only teaches a good curriculum but also is morally conscious as far as behavior and respect for others." ***Sheila Burton, Parent***

"*Step by Step Phonics* has been the backbone of my spelling program for two years. It is a very simple, yet effective program built around a balanced approach to literacy using repetition, poetry, good literature, and writing."
Gale C. Ortega, First/Second Grade Teacher
University of LaVerne: MA Degree

"*Step by Step Phonics* is a practical, sound, comprehensive guide to the teaching of phonics including a strong partnership with writing and language."
Pearle Ludwig, Lifelong Teacher, 35 years
Worcester Teachers College: MA Degree

"...A lot of good material in *Step by Step Phonics*. I thought the Eight Guidelines for Total Reading Success exceptional!"
Peg Hildar Coen, *ESL Tutor*
Moorhead State University, MN

"*Step by Step Phonics* provided me with a straight forward spelling program that had meaning. The program is simple, systematic, and successful."
Sandra McKenna, First Grade Teacher
University of San Diego